DUNCAN B. MEDILL

ROBERT B. MEDILL

—Photographs taken in 1897

Klondike Diary

True account of the Klondike rush of 1897 - 1898

by

Robert B. Medill

Portland, Oregon

Beattie and Company

1949

Dedicated to
Truth Seekers
Everywhere

INTRODUCTION

Robert B. Medill was born in a log cabin in Ohio, the son of Scotch-Irish parents and one of a family of nine living children.

His father was a miner, and at nine years of age Robert was taken into the mines. He was not able to do any particular amount of work, but his name on the payroll allowed his father a few more cars to fill and added a few more dollars to the monthly pay check. Thus his boyhood school days were rudely ended.

As was the custom among miners in those days, all the boy's wages were turned over to his mother. He had very little spending money of his own. I remember his telling me of three dollars and fifty cents he had when he was about seventeen which he spent for books.

He attended night school whenever the opportunity presented itself. After he was twenty-one, he carefully saved his earnings and attended college, completing a business course and also a teacher's course. Part of the latter was completed after he and I were married.

His brother's life followed about the same pattern except in the choice of studies. Duncan took a course in mining engineering from the Scranton, Pennsylvania, School of Mines, and at the time of the Klondike excitement he was superintendent of the Mattheson and Hegeler coal mine at LaSalle, Illinois.

The meager teacher's salary of those days, even with the low cost of living, was not enough to support a family and made it necessary for us to add to our income in other ways. As married women were not allowed to teach, I did dressmaking. I continued at this the year my husband was gone.

The poor financial condition of many families was one cause of the stampede to the gold fields of the Klondike. My husband and his brother were not first from our neighborhood to go. One man we knew did not return and was never heard from again. What happened to him no one ever knew.

i

At first my husband's letters came quite frequently, but after the two men reached Dyea the letters were few and far between. If the men met someone coming out, they always sent a letter for me. The last one sent in this manner was the one my husband gave to Swiftwater Bill in October. By the time Swiftwater had carried the letter in his pocket to Seattle, the envelope was completely worn out, and the letter itself had a hole through it. He put it in a new envelope, and I received it in December.

In June, I received a whole packet of letters which had been held up at different places. Some of these were just single sentences on leaves torn from his notebook; others were page after page of a large tablet. These letters were copied by M. C. O'Bryne, a lawyer of LaSalle, Illinois, and published in the LaSalle newspaper.

These letters and papers and my husband's diary, as well as many other interesting items, such as the contract drawn up by Judge Osborne of Seattle, in which he used ink made by dropping nail filings in vinegar, are still in my possession. All are documentary evidence of the truth of this book.

After their safe return, we were glad the two brothers had made the trip. If they had not, we would always have regretted a lost opportunity. In several of his letters my husband remarked that he would not h a v e missed the experience for anything.

Upon his return he again took up teaching, but the salary, even of principal and later of superintendent of Oglesby schools, was not sufficient to induce him to remain in that occupation. He tried his luck at various jobs, operating a lumber yard in Oklahoma, farming in Montana and Canada, but he was always happiest when teaching. One place in Montana he held an Indian school in an old log house erected by Angus McDonald of Hudson Bay Company fame and had some of McDonald's grandchildren as pupils.

Our final move was to Oregon where we lived for more than twenty-five years. Of this time my husband put in four years teaching in a CCC Camp. He often said these four years were the happiest years of his life. He was back at the job he loved—teaching, especially adults —though some of them had to be taught as children.

The boys in this Camp all came from the South, and of every contingent of two hundred boys there would be about thirty who could neither read nor write. Some could not even count. Thus his classes ranged from the very beginners to high school students.

These boys were all very anxious to learn and so grateful for the opportunity that he felt his life was not a failure here. He was accomplishing some good. I shall cite one instance:

A young man who, when he came, could not read nor write and who had no idea what counting meant, in one year's time was the proud possessor of an eighth grade diploma granted by the county superintendent of schools. Words could not express that young man's gratitude. All the boys were benefited more or less, and they all loved their teacher whom they lovingly called 'Pop.'

After the Camp closed, there followed two years of teaching American Citizenship.

We never found the "Pot of Gold" but we became rich in memories, in experiences, and in friends.

And now we come to "Klondike Diary." My husband and his brother always intended writing it together, but they were too busy making a living. It was one of the things easy to put off. Not until almost his seventieth year did my husband find time and leisure to go over all his notes and get this material into book form. By that time Duncan was gone. Having to retrace all the trails of this momentous journey with only his brother's ghost for a companion caused my husband many pangs of grief.

We found it necessary to type the manuscript ourselves. We bought a typewriter and a book of instructions and learned the touch system and found a lot of satisfaction and pleasure in being able to do this work without help.

Death claimed him before the book was published, and, now that the work is being done, I am saddened by the thought that he is not here to enjoy the pleasure and satisfaction that is the reward of a duty well done.

May you who read this book see those men—forty thousand of them—as they actually were, fighting mud, rain, snow, and ice, slipping, sliding, falling over rocks, and trees, facing the bitter cold and starvation a n d death! For what? For gold? Only for what gold would enable them to do: provide better living conditions for their families, give them schooling and comforts that many of them had been denied.

Mary A. Medill

I

OFF TO SEATTLE

We shall keep to the truth and nothing but the truth in relating our experiences in the Klondike gold rush— a homely narrative of a gigantic undertaking. We shall endeavor to set forth what happened to those who arrived and those who departed, those who gathered gold and those who did not—the multitudinous daily experiences of the gold seekers.

It would seem unnecessary to set down here anything about the extent and magnitude of the excitement created throughout the world and especially in the United States by the gold strike in the Klondike. We, who were living during those exciting days and were caught in the great cloud of gold fever germs that emanated from the north and bred a thousand fold in the fertile field of propaganda throughout the world, we can never forget.

But that was fifty years ago, and to those who have grown up since then and to whom the word 'Klondike' has no special meaning, and to the generations that will follow, this Klondike Diary may prove of interest.

Here was the opportunity for which the great mass of have-nots had been waiting: gold in unlimited quantities for merely sticking a pick into the ground. Didn't George McCormac, Swiftwater Bill, King Alec McDonald, and many others just push their shovels into the ground and countless thousands poured forth? Didn't Ole Olson and everybody else run out with their picks and dig out nuggets as big as their fists? "Anyone can do the same anywhere all over that country!"

Many about us were reported going or gone, among whom were friends and acquaintances. Naturally, brother Duncan and I who had known poverty and hardship, got the fever, at first, only a r a s h, then the real thing. Brother was manager of the Mattheson and Hegeler coal mine at LaSalle, Illinois; I was teaching one of the Ogles-

1

by schools across the Illinois river and owned a photograph studio in LaSalle.

We had struggled for years to find something better than digging coal, with the above mentioned small successes. But our financial success was still in the offing, and might it not be this gold field was the opportunity knocking at our door?

At the same time neither of us was in the best of health, and the roughing would kill or cure—cure, of course, we thought. Duncan was about six feet tall and weighed two hundred and ten pounds. I was five feet and nine inches tall but weighed only one hundred and thirty-two pounds. Neighbors assured me that I would never stand the trip, that I would die on the trail.

Duncan was leaving a wife and three children and I, a wife and two little ones. It was not easy to decide on such a trip under the conditions. But we finally gave up our jobs, packed up, and hit the trail August 20, 1897.

A friend at LaSalle gave us a letter of introduction to a friend of his in Chicago who would save us money on our trip to Seattle—he did. This Chicago friend in turn, gave us a letter to Dr. Crewe of Chicago, who had, the week before, lectured on the gold fields of Alaska and was now on his way to the Klondike, having preceded us by a few days.

In Chicago, we ran into Montgomery Ward's store to purchase a part of our outfit. We arrived at Ward's about one-thirty Saturday afternoon and found only Mr. Ward at the store as they closed afternoons on Saturdays. Mr. Ward called one of his men from a proposed sail on Lake Michigan—I think he was Mr. Thorne—to wait on us. He gave us very friendly service.

That evening we left for Seattle.

The trip to Seattle was of little moment except for one thing. Soon after leaving Chicago one of our fellow travelers learned our reason for traveling and quizzed us to death, almost. Not only that but he spread the news throughout the car, "Those boys are headed for Dawson!"

One fat old duffer down the aisle, upon hearing the news, said with a groan, "God help them!" Before we were across the plains, we had to set up a backfire of lies to save ourselves.

While we were still in North Dakota, the food my wife had packed to last us clear to Seattle was gone. We were making a brave start and arrived in Seattle in good condition.

We found no discouragement in Seattle. This town of thirty to forty thousand was all Klondike. We had no doubt it was in the pay-streak. Great streamers were stretched across the streets, screaming in lurid colors, Klondike this, and Klondike that. The town was full of strangers with the Klondike look in their faces. Horses and burros were led through the streets bearing "For Sale" signs. The argonauts were getting all the attention,

We had dinner, then began to gather our outfit.

"We don't want any beans!" No, beans were not for us. Neither of us would eat beans at home, and we did not care to pack them seventeen hundred miles to Dawson.

"But," said the clerk, "You'll find beans the staff of life in that cold country. You must take beans, or you"ll be sorry."

"Sure!" every one said, "You must take beans!"

We capitulated. "All right, put in four fifty-pound sacks."

Having our food supply taken care of , we went to the shipping office and took passage on the "Willamette," a 225-foot steamer, to leave Saturday. We bought two ponies for delivery in the morning, then secured a room on the sixth floor of the Price Hotel. From there we could see the "Willamette" at her dock loading up.

When we arose the next morning and were dressing, we heard the hoofs of a galloping horse down on the plank pavement below. I looked out the window and saw a dashing woman on a dashing horse. She was in riding breeches and riding astride, the first woman I had ever seen riding so. She and her horse made a beautiful sight.

When we went in for our first meal at Seattle, the waiter said, "What part of the country do you boys come from?"

Surprised by the question, we queried, "Why do you ask?"

"I know you don't belong on the coast because of your sunburn. No one gets a tan like that here."

By Friday, the twenty-seventh, we had bought another pony and had brought everything over to the dock. What a sight that dock warehouse was! Outfits for two hundred men, all standing in separate piles, six to eight feet high, like so many sentries, standing at attention. White sacks of flour and meal were crossed in pairs to the top. Odd boxes and sacks of clothing leaned about the bottom of the piles, all bearing the names of the owners.

The steamer "Topeka" pulled out that day for the north, loaded down with Klondikers and their belongings. She was a fine boat.

As we strolled about, we ran into Dr. Crewe and his party. We presented our letter of introduction, and he received us very graciously. He introduced us to his two companions whose names I do not find in my notes. One, about thirty years old, quite fat, Doc. nick-named "Tubby," which the young man seemed to resent. The other was about thirty-five, quiet and business-like.

Dr. Crewe was a large, raw-boned, blustering, self-contained, know-it-all kind of man. He was going in light, only one thousand pounds of outfit for three men. He would reach Dawson in three weeks and make a strike on the American side richer than the Klondike! So he said. He had shot Miles' canyon and White Horse Rapids but would not do it again. He would have a light boat and portage. The three men booked on the "Willamette" with us.

We went aboard the "Willamette" Saturday afternoon and watched the final loading of the ship. Each outfit was dumped into a net on the dock and hoisted up into the air by power applied to a large crane, swung over a large hatch in the deck, and lowered away down into the bottom of the hold, where it was released. All the outfits were dumped down there in a great heap. Then, by the same crane, with a box attached to the cable, the two hundred horses were landed on the second floor below the deck and placed in the stalls. This box, by means of which the horses were loaded, was built to hold one horse, and the horses were loaded in rapid succession. The forty steers were handled in a different manner, in a way one would never forget.

Visualize the ship on flood tide, standing twelve feet, or nearly that, higher than the dock. The steers were to be loaded up over the side of the ship and lowered down two decks below the top deck. A gangway, a kind of stair shute, leaned from the dock against the top of the ship's side for the steers to walk up, but it was too steep for them to climb. On lower tide they could have done so, but not now. Did this bother the ship's crew? Not for a minute. All of those large steers had big horns, and as each one was crowded through a narrow fence affair to the bottom of the shute, a large rope was clamped about the base of the horns. Away went the steer up into the air; he was swung over the deck and lowered down into the ship. When they were picked up by the horns, those poor animals had the fright of their lives. Theirs necks bulged out; the cords stood out like large ropes; their eyes were full of terror; their four legs stood straight out, quivering as if it were their last moment of life. Thanks to efficiency, it was over in a moment, and they didn't seem to have been hurt.

We were called to s u p p e r at six o'clock and got another eye full: a table, so long one could hardly see the farther end, at which two hundred men were seated. The table was piled with potatoes roasted with their jackets on, bread, butter, several kinds of meat, all in tin or granite containers, tin plates and cups. Plenty of substantial food, but no style.

At nine-thirty we steamed away from Seattle across the sound. We awoke the next morning tied up at Port Townsend, left Townsend at eleven and tied up at Victoria at three twenty-five where we lay till eight. During our stay at Victoria we rode the street car to the end of the line, visited the new Parliament building under construction, visited several stores, principally to hear the English dialect spoken by the girl clerks.

Next morning we pulled into Departure Bay docks where we took on coal. As we ran into the bay, we were looking at a fishing boat and wondering if the boys were having any luck. We had no suspicion that the "boys" were talking about us, but they were. One of them said, "Wouldn't be surprised if the Medill boys are on that boat." Soon after we tied up, the fishing boat came under full sail gracefully around our bow and tied up to the dock. Five or six men got out on the dock, but we paid them no further attention. Soon after, pushing through the crowd on the deck, came an old friend, Jim Curry, from our home town in Illinois. Behind Jim came a bunch of brawny Scots, all miners at Nanaimo. Having an idle day, they had been out fishing to pass the time. Jim had received a letter saying, "The Medills are on the way!" His surmise that we might have been aboard the "Willamette" proved correct. We had a nice visit, and they wished us luck as they left the ship.

I was intrigued by the beautiful scenery about the Sound, evergreen covered mountains and verdure. I left the ship and wandered two miles inland along a trail and enjoyed every step of the walk. The forest of strange trees, mostly evergreen, and the density of the undergrowth was almost impenetrable off the trail. I could almost see deer, bears, and such at every turn. As I did not want my boat to pull out and leave me, I did not spend a year there as I would like to have done. Others were more venturesome, however, and as a result, three of the Klondikers were left behind when the boat pulled out at eight. They had gone to Nanaimo, some eight miles. Thought they could make it back in time, but we never saw them again.

Tuesday morning I was awakened by water coming in on me through the port hole. It was raining, and the ship was doing a queer dance. It would roll to its right side, then angle up and roll to its left side and angle down. The swells, the first we had ever felt, were roaring along the ship's side, and curses were roaring along the bunks. I scrambled out and hurried along to the stairs to go on deck. I wanted to see what it was all about. Before I reached the stairs, I felt my body s h r i n k to half its height, then suddenly stretch to twice its height and repeat. My stomach took on the same gymnastics. I turned about and reached my bunk just in time to save my empty stomach from insulting my throat. In a short time we were in still water again. They told us we had been crossing the Dixon Entrance, where the ocean swells came rolling in. The strong wind had driven the rain and spray through the open portholes and sprinkled all the bunks.

It was a rainy day, obliging us to spend most of our time in our bunks. A young fellow struck up familiar tunes on his mandolin that with the gloom aroused more or less homesickness. But at noon we were all delighted to find the tables set with chinaware. Apparently we were to be trusted now since the rough water was past.

For several hundred miles, the constantly throbbing engines pushed the ship through narrow channels of exquisite beauty. To us tenderfeet, the channel seemed but one to two hundred yards wide. Beautiful mountains rose directly from the water's edge. We were passing through an evergreen canyon, usually green to the tops; but here and there peaks rose, bare or covered with snow, poking their heads up through clouds or into the blue, as the weather conditions changed. Here and there white cascades shimmered down through the green of the mountains' sides, while eagles soared from mountain top to mountain top across the channel.

During the nights, we passed a number of steamers going both ways. Their lights glimmering from ship and water were quite a sight. Occasionally, during the days, we saw Indians in their dark dugout canoes skulking along the shadowy shores. Schools of dolphins, salmon and other fishes, leaped from the water as they went sporting by. Time and distance passed quickly.

Thursday at three the engines stopped their perpetual grind, and for over an hour we stood at anchor. The crew said they were waiting the turn of the tide. From the demeanor of the officers I had a hunch they were uncertain which of two channels to take. However that might be, the next morning at six o'clock we tied up at Juneau and approached the city on our left.

Apparently we had circled Douglas Island during the night and were heading southeast. If that were so, I have never been able to figure out why we did not take the right hand channel the evening before and save the cruise clear around the island during the night.

We were tied up at Juneau five hours. It was a city of three thousand to thirty-five hundred people and so unusually situated it was a curiosity to all. A small patch of rough ground between the channel and foot of a high, bare, almost perpendicular mountain, supported the city of Juneau as a foundation. Industrially, it was supported by the Treadwell mines and mills across the channel on Douglas Island.

We pulled out from the Juneau dock and a few lengths from the dock were stuck in the mud. Yes, actually, stuck in the mud! The heavily loaded ship was drawing quite a depth of water, and she grounded on what appeared to be a clay bottom. She was stuck. No amount of chugging of the engines could take us through. The engines were shut off a few minutes and reversed. By a super effort, the ship moved back a few feet, then forward with all steam let loose. She hit the clay barrier cachug, and we all staggered forward in sympathy. This

8

process oft repeated did the trick, and we were again on our way, leaving a trail of clay-colored water behind us.

A little ways farther along the channel we moved over to the right shore and tied up to the dock at Treadwell. Here we were all invited to inspect the Stamp Mill. I have always been sorry we couldn't accept, but Duncan was not feeling well and could not go. As he was the mining engineer and would have enjoyed the experience most, I would not have been happy going without him. I did, however, enjoy watching a giant nozzle tear down the hill near the ship, the first I had ever seen.

We left Treadwell, and a short ways ahead we turned sharply to the right around the south-east end of Douglas Island. Soon, on our left, we passed a wonderful glacier. We kept to the right side of the channel, opposite the glacier, and got one of the thrills of our trip. I can only guess that the vertical face of the ice was several hundred feet high above the water. A ship between us and the ice was small in comparison. Great segments of ice often broke loose and crashed down into the water as we passed, causing big waves, and the air was cold. I am sorry I haven't the name of the glacier, but I am sure it was not the Muir.*

We retired Friday night, conscious of the fact that we would reach the end of our steam-boat-trail on the morrow, as we had but ninety miles farther to go. We were getting our nerves set. We had asked for it, and it looked like we were going to get it.

*A letter from the Juneau Chamber of Commerce in 1938, forty years after this trip was made, says the name of the glacier was the "Taku."

9

II

LANDING AT DYEA

At six o'clock Saturday morning, September fourth, I was awakened by a loud creaking and clatter of chains. Dropping anchor! Scrambling into my clothes, I ran up on deck to find about fifty Klondikers ahead of me. The ship was standing crosswise of the channel, about one-quarter of a mile from shore, her nose pointing toward a dark valley. Like a parent sending his son out into the world she seemed to say, "There you are, son. This is as far as I can take you."

The various "sons" were standing forward quietly, looking toward the shore, while the other one hundred and fifty of them were coming on deck as quickly as the narrow hatchway would let them out.

"What's all the excitement?"

"Have we arrived?" Such were the questions as all the passengers came forward. The answers were as general and as significant.

"Well, there she is, boys! That's what you have been looking for! How does she look to you? Skagway on the right here, and Dyea on the left."

A queer shore line stretched before us. A range of hills, coming out at right angles to the channel, seemed to stop at sight of us, resting its forefeet in the water and leaning slightly back in surprise. On either side of this range are valleys whose outer sides are enclosed by other mountain ranges. Because of the overcast sky and early hour, the valleys were not inviting. One could easily imagine large, dripping, dismal signs stretching across their cavernous mouths, 'Enter here at your peril.'

Filled with the same emotions, enveloped in and held by the psychology of the moment, the whole two hundred Klondikers were soon on deck, gazing shoreward. It was a serious moment. Until now we had had assistance; railroads, ships, hotels. In comparison with what lay ahead, it seemed heaven. There before us lay two forbidding valleys. Up one lay the Skagway trail, and up the other lay the Chilkoot. Beyond there lay seven hundred and fifty miles of wilderness: mountains, lakes and streams filled with barriers and dangers. We are aware of the fact that when we leave the ship we are on our own. If we move a mile, move our outfit a mile, we do it of our own strength and ingenuity. It is a prospect most forbidding. All sense the gravity of the situation.

I want to commend the men who made up the passenger list of the "Willamette," or the Klondikers on board—I saw no women on the ship—those two hundred men were the finest body of men, physically and mentally, with which it was ever my privilege to associate. Many were university educated. All seemed above the average in every way. If any of them had any notions of staying with the ship and returning to civilization, it didn't show. There seemed to be but one impulse: jump ashore and tackle the dragon.

Word soon came around, "Captain says unloading cannot begin before tomorrow and maybe not then." Now what!

"We have just got to get off! Got seven hundred and fifty miles ahead and the river may freeze up before we arrive at Dawson!"

Seems like our mental reactions reached shore in telepathic waves, or a few harpies on shore winded their quarry, for directly a number of rowboats were skimming across the water toward the ship, each one carrying one to three men. They came alongside, threw their tie ropes up over the ship's rail where the nearest man made them fast. Other men threw down rope ladders that were hanging handy along the rail. Did you ever try to navigate a rope ladder on a ship's side?

Well, these harpies came aboard. I'll now call them pirates for each man had not only his whiskers but a complete pirate outfit—belt, gun, and knife. They wanted to look tough but succeeded only in looking ridiculous.

They got a reception of dignified contempt from the Klondikers. I'll warrant every Klondiker had a gun, too, but he was not parading it. But directly there was one exception.

The chubby young man in Dr. Crewe's company couldn't resist the impulse from his natural sense of humor. He came on deck dressed as a take-off on the pirates. He had four guns and a knife bristling from his person. Two guns in his belt, one protruding from each boot leg, and a bowie knife resting snugly between his belt and protruding paunch. With never a word and the gravest face, he swaggered up and down the deck. Of course, it brought a big laugh and broke the tension.

The pirates got busy. "You fellows want to get your outfits ashore? You may be here two weeks before the ship's crew unloads your stuff."

"Yes, surely, what will you charge?"

"The minimum is seventy-five dollars and up."

"Yeah! You don't want much."

"Well, pardner, you'll not get off for any less."

The pirates spread out among the Klondikers, keeping their ears cocked to learn if any outsider dared to butt in on their game.

Later, a canoe came alongside, and a large serious man came up over the side. He had no guns or other arms. He was dressed in cap, tight fitting jacket, and hip gum boots. He appeared to be just a casual visitor, but the pirates were onto him. Two or three hung about him continually. Duncan got next to him somehow pretty soon and brought him to me, saying, "Here is a man who says he will deliver our outfit over at Dyea for twenty dollars." As Dyea was four miles over there—to us uninitiated it didn't look a mile—I was somewhat surprised.

I said, "Horses, too?"

"No, just the outfit without the horses."

"Well, seems fair enough. When can you do it?"

"Soon as you can get the stuff out of the hold."

We agreed to avail ourselves of his services.

The pirates soon had the word that an honest ferry man was among us. What an uproar, swaggering and cussing! "Any blankety, blank, blank who would cut prices will be strung up!" They were closing in on our man and getting abusive, not directly to him, but to all and sundry. It finally got too uncomfortable for our friend, and he threw his leg over the rail and disappeared over the side of the ship into his canoe. He took up a paddle and was soon on shore.

The pirates were loud in their expletives. "By the blankety blank, blank, he better go while the going's good."

In about half an hour who comes up over the side of the ship but our friend, quietly, slowly, majestically. He wears a belt and gun. He walks leisurely about the deck. The pirates are in a huddle at the far end of the ship. They scowl, they grunt to each other, they clamber over the ship's side and pull to shore. Guess their squaws were calling them.

Sometime before noon Duncan told me there was a husky young fellow on board trying to find some one to feed him to Dawson for his help. He had come up from Seattle without an outfit, and broke, in the hopes of getting to the gold fields on this basis. We considered it awhile then dropped the matter. The thought of parting with a considerable portion of our grub did not appeal to us at the moment. But after dinner—midday meal always —we fell to discussing our prospect of finding the river frozen up before we reached Dawson and got back to discussing our neighbor's help. Perhaps the time gained by his help would be the very thing to insure our reaching our destination before the freeze-up. That is just what happened.

Duncan knew the man and went in search of him. Returning shortly, he introduced Harry Reese, Norwegian, thirty-four years old, weight, one-hundred and sixty-five pounds, five feet eight inches tall. With a friendly grin and "By gar" he was glad to join us.

"All right, Harry, stand pat and stand by. Things will be happening soon."

"Aw right, by gar, I stand pat," was about the conversation that took place.

In the afternoon, some of the boys going the Skagway trail made some arrangement to have their horses taken off the ship. The big doors or hatches on the first and second decks were opened. Using the same power crane and horse box used at Seattle to load them, they soon had a horse coming up from below. They hoisted the horse almost up to the peak of the crane, then swung it out over the water. T h e y lowered the box to within twelve to sixteen feet of the surface.

By some mechanical arrangement, the door in front of the box fell away on hinges, the box was slowly canted at the rear end, and the horse was plunged into the channel. It disappeared but soon came to the surface fighting. It swam to the side of the ship, poor thing, but finding no place in the side of the big black hull to place its feet, turned away facing the western shore. The land was too far away to encourage it, or it could not see the land. It swam in a circle till it faced the Skagway shore, then, stretching out its beautiful neck and body in a horizontal position, the water lapping over its back, it struck out straight for shore. It swam quite gracefully and swiftly and soon had reached a point about two-thirds the distance to shore where its hind feet touched bottom. We could tell this by the upward heave of its hips. Soon it was half side out of water w h e r e it stopped several minutes to rest, then, continuing, was soon out on dry land . We all heaved a sigh of relief. We had all been suffering as well as the horse. But we had seen nothing yet.

The next horse was dumped out sooner and somewhat higher above the water. It came up slower and began pawing the water with its front feet and seemed to be struggling for breath. It, too, approached the side of the ship only to be discouraged. Its great lustrous eyes were full of terror, and we were glad when it turned toward

Skagway. But we were relieved only for a moment, for we soon perceived that nature had not been so kind to this horse in the matter of swimming as its predecessor. It was soon pawing the air, front feet coming out of the water at each stroke and making little headway. Directly, it was in an almost vertical position; head, neck and shoulders out of the water, and seemed to be trying to climb up into the air. In fact, it seemed in its last struggle and would go down stern first, directly. A roar of alarm rang along the deck. "That horse is going to drown!"

There seem to be heroes for every occasion. Some spring into the breach while others stand helpless. Two forms slid over the ship's side, plumped into a rowboat, and shot through the water. As the skilled oarsman drove the boat by the side of the floundering beast, the man in the rear reached out and grasped the dangling halter rope, braced his feet, and by one deft movement brought the horse's head over the rear deck and held it tight. The poor beast again had reason to trust in man. It laid its head on the deck, stretched out its body horizontally, and swam as it should have done in the first place, but didn't know how. We did not cheer, but I am sure a profound feeling of relief passed through all the spectators. The two men soon had him to the place where he could stand half side up, threw him the halter rope, and returned to the ship.

That horse was surely spent; it was fully half an hour before he got strength enough to crawl up the bank. Several more were landed without difficulty, all having to swim. They would have been better off, however, if they had drowned. They would have been saved much misery, because they, with the rest of the two hundred with few exceptions, would be dead in two weeks.

I feel sure the fate of horses on those trails gave pain to the Klondikers the rest of their lives.

During the afternoon, some men came from Skagway and announced they would transport horses to Dyea at six dollars per head. We were fortunate to get in on this.

Late in the afternoon they brought a big scow alongside and loaded nine horses, two burros, and about five tons of feed stuff. Duncan and Harry went along to care for our horses and feed. They had not left the ship far till they were swallowed up by darkness. I felt lonely. I had remained behind to look after our outfit and help the boat-man get it to Dyea in the morning. He had hung around all day, but we had been unable to get our goods out of the hold. I slept on deck that night. In the morning, after breakfast, I went in search of the Captain.

After some rambling about, I found him and asked him if he would get our goods on deck as we had a boat coming for them. He looked very serious, and after a moment replied, "I can't do a thing for you." Then, with a grin, he added, "My whole crew of stevedores deserted last night for the gold fields, and I have no men for the job."

For a moment I was stumped. But immediately I plyed him with another question, "Can I get the stuff out myself?"

"You can try," pointing to a windlass bolted to the deck near the big hatch.

"All right!" I said, and began pulling at the doors. He gave me a hand, and, going below, he had the lower deck doors opened. I pulled slack rope from the drum and let it dangle down, away down, to the great pile of outfits for two hundred men in the bottom of the ship. Some one said, "There's a net," and I saw a net go floating down on the pile of goods. I looked up to see the ship's engineer. I thanked him.

I thought to go down, affix the net full of goods, come up, and wind them up. Just then a young man, about twenty-five years of age, came forward with a pained, eager look on his face, and said, "What are you going to do?"

"I am going to get my stuff on deck. I've got a boat coming for it directly."

"May I get mine up too?"

16

"Good! You wind for me, and I'll wind for you."

I took a turn of the rope around my foot, and slid away down on top of the mountain of bags and boxes. I looked around and for a moment was at a loss just how to find our stuff amongst all that pile. I looked around over the top of the pile and was delighted to find one bag with our name on it. That indicated our goods had gone in among the last, and would, no doubt, be pretty much together. That was so, and I soon had the net full and checked them on the list in my book. The young man on the windlass hoisted them all on deck, and I hoisted his. He was as fortunate as I, in having his goods go in on top of the pile. By the time we got our goods up there were a number of men hunting over the pile, and I suppose the windlass was kept busy all day.

I had not long to wait. My boat was along directly, and we passed the goods down in the net by the same windlass and were off.

My boatman had a very handsome boy along with him. He was dressed in a light sombrero, buckskin jacket, and tight fitting blue overalls. What was my surprise in landing in the boat to be introduced to the handsome boy as the boatman's wife. About the second time I had ever seen a woman in man's trousers.

Could I have looked ahead thirty years, I would not have been quite so embarrassed. I would have been able to notice her beautiful black eyes and hair, the sweet cut of her oval cheek, the clear olive skin, the rich bud of a mouth, and all the other charms of her sweet physical and spiritual personality. But far was it from me at that time to make such an appraisal. Was I not the virtuous father of two children who had a most wonderful mother?

The boatman ran up the sail and for awhile it seemed to work all right. But soon the wind whipped around and the sail had to come down. I was asked to take an oar on one side while the wife took the opposite. Her husband took an oar over the stern. An oar over the stern, in the

17

hands of an expert, will apply more power than two oars on the sides, and this man was an expert.

He stood up. With a goodly portion of the oar above the lock and with a back and forth swing of his body, his weight went on to the oar at each swing. With a deft, mysterious cant to the blade at each stroke, I could feel the boat move forward. This is called sculling. He made four strokes to our one and was the real motive power. We did our bit, of course, but I am obliged to confess that because of my run-down condition mentioned before, I had all I could do to hold my own with the little woman on the other oar.

During the early part of our trip, when things were not so strenuous, these folks confided to me that they were from the state of Arizona. I at once classified them as of Spanish and Russian descent. She was a dark beauty and he, a large, rather handsome blonde. Both spoke good American with no foreign accent, and I concluded they were both native Americans.

We got to the place where the wind forsook us and the backwash of the tide was with us in all its cussedness. We rowed and we sculled. We blistered our hands, and while I wanted to quit and let her drift, I was ashamed to so much as show a sign of my weakness. The little woman opposite was doing as much as I with never a complaint. What would men ever do without the encouragement of women!

We worked our way across the tide and Dyea shore to the farther shore where the mountain comes plumping down into the water, thinking the current might be less powerful close to that rocky shore line. But each powerful surge we gave the boat seemed to gain but an inch. "How long, how long can I stand this!" was running through my mind.

After what seemed the longest nightmare of my life, we gained the Dyea beach, where the sand comes down. For four hours we had used every ounce of our strength on those oars, not relaxing for one second, and my soft hands were a sight. There I learned the strength of a falling tide, and the next June I met the gentleman again, as we were navigating the channel around Michael's Island and I'd had enough foolishness. Drifting with the tide has some virtue.

We ran the boat along the shore front from the left side of the valley till we reached the Dyea river on the right. There we tried to stem the river current, but as it was too much for us and commenced to carry us down, I dropped my oar and went over into the water, only about three feet deep near shore, and pulled the boat to shore.

We soon located the boys who brought a horse down to the boat to tow us up the stream.

They said, "What kept you so long?"

"Kept us so long!" I cried, with my r e m a i n i n g strength.

"What time next year is this?"

They hooked the horse rope to the boat and towed it up stream to a good landing where we cached the goods. The word 'cached' means concealed stored goods, but in the Yukon country the goods were rarely ever concealed. They were never molested.

While we were cooking and eating, Duncan told me what had happened to them after they moved away from the ship into the darkness with the horses.

They had had a heck of a time. They got before the Dyea shore at low tide where they cast anchor for two hours, while, in the darkness, it rained on them all the while. They thought with the incoming tide to attempt a landing, but the tide, having a long shore to ramble upon, wouldn't stop rambling for just a bunch of Klondikers. They couldn't make the scow stay put. It kept floating from its bearings. As the boys got some of the load off, the boat would move away. That was not the worst thing. They found the tide reaching, always reaching for the feed they had cached on the sandy shore. They could not see the high tide mark in the darkness,

19

and every little while what had been unloaded had to be moved farther and farther up. It was three o'clock in the morning before they got everything above high tide mark. Then, pitching the tent, they lay down to sleep in wet clothes on the wet ground. This was but an initiation.

III

THE GREAT TREK BEGINS

After the rain and foggy weather of Saturday night, Sunday was clear. The sun shone all day, a comfort to us.

With everything landed on the shore of the Dyea stream, we settled our bill and chatted with the boatman and his wife. We later bid them good-bye and watched them as they were hurried by the current down to the bay, where they disappeared around the mountain side. Gone into the mists of time from which they had so suddenly appeared, typical of all human contacts.

We moved the goods above high water mark near the timber, but still on sandy soil. We started a fire and made some dinner. According to my notes of the date, I must have been nearly famished: "Made some coffee, ate half a loaf. Quit for shame's sake."

Up to this time of our lives, we had seen little or nothing of those children of the wilderness, the American Indians. Naturally, we were curious about them. That is, I was. Brother had formed a prejudice against them before we had seen any.

I had not long to wait, for who should come walking down the trail and over to our camp-fire, but two squaws, each bearing a large pack on her back. They pushed the bands of the packs from their foreheads and dropped the packs on the sand. Without a word, they untied their bundles and spread out an assortment of buckskin moccasins, gloves, caps and other articles, and then squatted on the sand as only a squaw can. I asked them what price they had on the various articles; the younger, and much more comely of the two, answered me in good English. After the purchase of some moccasins and gloves, I asked her why the other w o m a n didn't say anything. She answered, "My mother does not speak English."

"How come you do, but she doesn't?"

"I went to school at Juneau."

21

"Then you can read and write?"

"Yes."

I gave her a letter written in longhand which she read and said, "That is a nice letter."

Down the trail came an uncouth looking white man. He stopped and spoke to the squaws in their language, and a quarrel seemed to ensue. Duncan got dark in the face. I could see he was about to tell him to move on. I saved the day by asking the man where he learned the Indian language. He said, "I have a Sleeping Dictionary."

Along the trail came two Indian young men dressed neatly in white man's clothes. Harry hailed them and waved for them to come over. As they approached he said, "Let me sell you a pair of fine boots."

The Indians looked down at a boot gravely, where Harry had thrown it down on the sand, and asked, "How much?"

Harry replied, "Twenty dollars."

"Huh, too much!"

"Too much! Say, do you see the fine leather in those boots?"

"Huh, we can get the same boot for seven-fifty from Montgomery Ward."

Monday, we packed our three ponies, took packs on our backs, and, leading the ponies, proceeded up the trail through Dyea. Dyea was a scattering of tents and two or three log shacks. Most of the inhabitants were Indians; a few white men seemed to belong. Then over in the forest at the foot of the mountain, perhaps one-fourth mile, there was an Indian village of five hundred Indians—so I was told—I didn't go over to see. I was told, also, that the Indians had formed a branch of the Salvation Army. We could hear singing over there in the evening.

One evening, so the story went, some of the Klondikers were present at the Salvation Army meeting. They failed to remove their hats but were shocked into consciousness by the Indians' shouting, "You white men take off your hats! You should be ashamed when we do much better."

We led the packed ponies up the trail about one and one-half miles to the first ford of the river, or ferry, depending on the mood of the stream. There, near the water's edge on the gravel, we cached the packs. The stream being low, a great expanse of gravel ran up to the timbered bank on our side; the far bank was abrupt. As I began to take the packs off two of the ponies, an Indian boy, about ten, came up and wanted to hold them. I gave him the halters, wondering what he would ask in payment.

After unpacking, he put his two hands up on the back of one pony and held up his foot. Just so, he wanted to ride. I gave him a boost, and he went galloping down the trail.

He soon returned saying, "You geet one." He wanted me to ride the other pony, probably to run a race.

I shook my head, and he went galloping off again to the great admiration of his playmates along the trail. I led the other pony along, soon coming to a group of Indian children playing in the sand. There seemed to be some dissension in the group. One little chap arose with clenched fists, flinging some apparent taunt at another. The other arose, too, with fists full of sand, and as they faced each other, the second boy flung his two handfuls of sand in the first boy's eyes, and ran away amidst the shrieks of the group. You have seen the same thing done among white children.

By late noon we had every thing up to the ferry. We were preparing dinner, and I could not find the salt. A large man came across the gravel from the direction of a tent perched upon the bank among the trees. As he came forward, I was still hunting for the salt and complaining.

He jerked his thumb over his shoulder and said, "Go up to the haythin in the tint and get some salt."

I looked at him a moment, and asked, "Is that your tent?"

He said, "Yis."

I picked up a cup and went toward the tent. As I did so, I noticed a comely squaw sitting in the doorway. I approached and said, "The man down there said I might get some salt from you."

She rose without a word and brought me the cup about a third full. I thanked her and returned. Later this squaw came down across the gravel with a pail. Her husband went to meet her, took the pail, and, in his hip boots, walked out into the stream, dipped the pail full of water and returned it to her.

While eating dinner, I asked this nice, big Irishman if we could ford the stream. He said we could, but he would ferry us over for a trifle. We made that arrangement, and, while it was being carried out, I made a final trip back through Dyea.

As I passed down the trail, I came upon a large group of Indian men and women. The men were sitting in a circle on the ground, and one woman was in the circle, standing up. With many gestures and much voice, she seemed to be belaboring another woman, who was standing outside the circle. Standing out beyond, were many men, women and children, with a number of white men. I stopped, of course, wondering what it was all about. The second woman walked into the circle, as the first one walked out. She began to flail her arms, and, raising her voice, shook her finger and fist at number one. I asked a white man what it was all about and he said, "They are having a trial." I would have given a great deal to know what they said.

I had noticed with interest the many beautiful boats of these Indians, had seen them all along the coast. They were all dugouts, carved from tree logs, and all stained a dark color. They seemed perfect to me, and here there were many.

THE GREAT TREK BEGINS

As I went down toward the river, I saw a canoe coming up the stream from the bay. It seemed to be the daddy of them all. There were about twenty Indian men in it. They were coming right along against the current, half the men on either side with a paddle each, and one at the stern with a long sweep. They were all standing up. They ran the prow on to the sandy shore. As it struck, the men leaped out in pairs, one pair after another, till all were out. As each pair struck the sand, the two would take hold of the boat and slide it upon the shore a part of its length, without a stop in its movement. As each pair reached a certain point, they loosed their holds on the boat and continued on up to Dyea without looking back.

Their whole set of movements, from the time they were using their paddles until they disappeared up the bank, was one continuous, unbroken rhythm of graceful, forceful movement. I stood entranced, watching this piece of skillful demonstration.

I then walked down to the boat, and, with the keenest interest and admiration, s t o o d and looked. Then I measured its length with out-stretched arms. It was forty-eight feet long, of a uniform width of six feet, and four and one-half feet deep. As far as I could judge it was perfect in line, thickness and workmanship. I asked the man who apparently stood guard where they got such a log to carve out such a boat. He said, "Down channel."

"Oh, yes." I said, "the trees are big down there."

Those familiar with west coast timber know that it was not necessarily from the largest tree. I asked him how much it was worth. He replied, "About two hundred dollars." I should say there was all of that much labor put on it.

IV

I MEET MRS. McLEAN

Monday night, September sixth, found us camped on the far side of the stream, at the ferry. Our tent was pitched on the high bank, with the door overlooking the stream, and I unrolled my sleeping bag with the head to the front of the tent.

I awoke at gray dawn, rolled over on my stomach, raised the bottom of the tent, and hooked it behind my head. I looked out on a most peaceful scene: a great stillness, the stream moving quietly along with patches of fog rising from its surface, a clear sky and a spring-like mildness.

I was enjoying the situation when my attention was called to a dark object coming from the trees on the farther shore. As it came slowly down the gravel, I made out a man, an I n d i a n. He had a long pole over his shoulder; he came down to the water's edge, directly across from me. Reaching the end of the pole out over the water, he pressed down till it touched the bottom of the stream, then gave it a sudden jerk toward himself, then another, and another jerk.

"What the Sam Hill is he trying to do?" I asked myself. I had seen no s u c h performance in my time. I watched him with all attention while he took a couple of steps carefully into the stream, reached his pole away out, and performed as he had before. He quietly moved forward again two steps and performed the same operation. He moved forward again, the water up to his thighs. At the second jerk, a new development took place. His pole seemed to have stuck. "No, by golly! There is something on the end of the pole, making it sway and tremble." He brought the pole across his stomach for leverage, and out of the water, stuck on the end of the pole, he raised a large fish. The fish went up into the air in an arch and landed out on the shore still attached to the

26

pole. The fisherman followed it out quite unconcernedly, apparently this was all in the day's struggle for existence. He removed the fish from the end of the pole, held it in his left hand, threw the pole over his shoulder with his right hand, and disappeared into the forest.

"Well, I"ll be darned, that fellow has breakfast for his whole family while we wise guys are still abed," I remarked to myself.

There I had an expanation of a thing that had excited my curiosity coming through Dyea. I had seen many long poles leaning against trees and over the sides of tents. They looked like long, strong fishing poles, but the interesting part was a large hook fastened to the end of the poles. The hooks were three or four inches between point and shank. I couldn't figure out their purpose till I saw that man obtain his breakfast. But since I have come to live on the Pacific coast, I have seen the white man fish for salmon in this manner. Probably he borrowed the trick from his Indian brother.

Getting back to the problem in hand, we soon had camp broken and with two hundred pounds on each pony, Harry and I went on up the trail toward Finnegan's Point. Duncan was to follow with the balance in a wagon which we had engaged for the purpose. Finnegan's Point was four and a half miles away, and the end of the wagon trail.

Always studying our maps and mileage and picking up what information we could from those we met on the trail, about what to expect ahead, we were usually fore-armed.

Knowing we would ford the stream several times, beyond the Point, and, as we meant to try to reach the entrance to the Canyon, I had pulled on hip gum boots, to my grief later.

At the Point, we rested till the wagon came up and unloaded. At this time, among those passing up and down the trail, came a young Indian buck with pack-straps on his pack, going back empty. He stopped suddenly and came up to me in a state of excitement. Looking at one of the ponies, he said, "How much for pony?"

"It's not for sale," I said.

"Will you take one hundred dollars?"

"No, but if you will be at the foot of the pass when we are through packing, I'll let you have her for fifteen dollars."

"Aw right! I get her. Sure now, you keep her for me?"

"Well, you'll have to be there. In that case, she is yours."

"Aw right, I be there!"

He was packing on the trail for pay, and, no doubt, making big money.

There was no surprise to me in his wanting that pony. There was not another like her on the trail. She was pure white and plump, with long, wavy mane and tail, and a most beautiful sheen. She looked as if she had just come out of a circus bandbox. The other two were black, and all were of the strong, wiry, western type.

Every horse on the trail was supplied with the common pack-saddle. They resemble nothing so much as a small saw-buck. They are set on the horses' backs, have breast and hip straps to hold them from sliding forward or backward, and are cinched down tight by two belly bands. Then, with a long rope, the packs are made secure.

We packed the ponies again, and Harry and I went forward to the mouth of the canyon. Sometimes following the trail, sometimes taking along the stream on the gravel or sand by fording back and forth.

When we reached the canyon's mouth, which is a narrowing of the valley, we cached our packs on the left side of the stream just outside the canyon. Here was a high, wide sand bar or bench.

My feet were so sore from the nine and one-half miles walk in the big gum boots, I pulled them off and returned in my socks. Where the trail got too rough for my feet, I rode the pony, perched in the pack-saddle.

On one of these stretches, I saw ahead of me what I took to be a boy, riding as I was. He was wearing some kind of red silk turban for a cap, a brown sweater, blue overalls and heavy boy's shoes. I wasn't interested. But by and by I heard him say, "John!" to his horse. There was no mistaking the voice, this was a woman with a pack horse alone on the trail.

On our return trip, Duncan and I were making the trip, and Harry remained with the stuff at the Point. As I came along, I found her in trouble. The packs had slid from her horse, and she was unable to replace them. I led my pony off the trail and helped her repack the horse. Of course she was grateful and thanked me over and over.

When we reached the canyon, I had made some nineteen miles of travel for the day, so I remained at the canyon, and Duncan returned with the three ponies, tied halter and tail. There were as many as thirty horses tied thus on the trail at times, two men handling the bunch.

Duncan and Harry were to bring up the remainder of the outfit that evening. The sun was still reaching me at the cache, and I had plenty of time to rest and write notes before their return. Of course, I would have to have a good supper ready for the boys. Duncan had had a fine dinner waiting for us at the Point on our return trip there. I had made the raise of a fine salmon and was getting it and some spuds ready to cook when, on looking up, there stood the woman holding her horse with empty pack saddle.

I had not heard her come forward on the sand and showed surprise. She laughed. We chatted awhile, and she told me her name was Mrs. McLean. Her husband was packing over the pass, making twenty-five dollars per day, and she was doing as well with her horse. She was French, she said, and her husband was Scotch. She was, perhaps, twenty-five to thirty years old, and quite good looking. I asked her to stay for supper, but she said she had too far to go. It would be dark before she reached Finnegan's Point.

I told her how I had taken her for a boy when I saw her ahead on the trail. She laughed again and said, "Yes, 'most everyone makes that mistake, but when my dresses wore out on the trail, there was nothing to do but take the handiest clothes I could get. You know, one day my horse got jambed with another horse in passing on the trail, and the man was going to slap me, when another man bawled out, 'You wouldn't strike a woman, would you?' You should have seen that fellow go off in confusion!"

She bid me good-bye and went off down the trail, and I turned my attention to getting supper.

Along about dark, I ate, the boys not having come. I then piled the outfit already there in two rows, about three feet apart, and spread the tent over them. I pulled my sleeping bag in under the tent, and later, as the boys didn't show up, I crawled into the bag. I didn't know a thing till about nine o'clock next morning, when I awoke and crawled out. The sun was up, and what was my surprise to see an addition to the cache. The boys had been there, but where were they? And the extra goods on the sand were only part of the stuff left down at the Point!

Directly the boys came back out of the canyon with the ponies empty. They had gone up there about half the canyon or three miles, with part of their packs, and returned, leaving their loads cached up there. They had dropped part of their loads as they went by, because of the reported hard trail in the canyon.

They were disgusted with me.

"Where the hell have you been? We came five miles without breakfast, and you are no place to be seen!"

"I was right there under the tent!"

"You couldn't have been, for we yelled and whistled our eyes out!"

I MEET MRS. McLEAN

"Can't help it, gentlemen, that's just where I was!"
You know, folks, I think they always questioned my veracity.

V.

THE CANYON AND SHEEP CAMP

Tuesday morning, the seventh, while waiting the reappearance of the boys, I wrote some flowery notes in my book about the grandeur of the scenery at the mouth of the canyon. Just as well I did, for it would be some time before I saw any more beauty.

That six miles of canyon cost us nearly everything but our shirts. It was one grand splash, slide, and tumble. Horses going down all along the trail. Ours went down off and on. Once, all three were down at the same time.

The canyon was a narrowing of the valley. The sides were steep and timbered, changing to steep and rocky the last two miles.

Some enterprising fellows had seen a Klondike right there. They had begun improving the trail by bridging ravines and corduroying bogs, charging tolls to those who crossed, and that meant everyone. It was impossible to go any other way. One poor fellow had tried to pass around one of those bridges just as I came up. He got his horse to the edge of the deep ravine, but it could not hold its footing, and went rolling and sliding to the bottom where it landed on its back, feet up. I thought he would have to shoot the horse where it lay, but he got it freed from its packs, got it onto its feet, and led it away down the ravine, gradually coaxing it up along the steep side and eventually coming out on top. Incidents of this kind were happening more often as we advanced, evidenced by the increasing number of dead horses we came upon.

We were Tuesday, Wednesday, Thursday and Friday battling in that canyon. The last two miles were the worst. To make matters worse, it rained Thursday and Friday. But by Friday night we had everything at Sheep

Camp. Everything was wet, of course, ourselves included, after two days in the rain.

What hit us the hardest was having no heat in the tent. We had been persuaded in Chicago that a little folding grate affair to go over the fire was the proper thing for lightness and usefulness in the way of a stove. In bringing it along we showed our inexperience. Not having a stove inside the tent, we wallowed in water, mud and slush.

Saturday we started out for the last three miles to the foot of the pass. We were getting worse trail fast. We got to Stonehouse, a large stone among the smaller stones or rocks. Why it was ever called Stone House is beyond me. That was as far as we thought it wise to go for one advance. It was two miles, and that was plenty f a r enough. We made it up and back, and it took us all day. It was the worst piece of trail in the whole Klondike trip. Up and down the rocks, into mud holes, horses and packs rolling down the mountain side.

On this piece of trail, where there was no timber, just brush and rock-slide on the mountain side, one of our horses rolled down among the rocks with four sacks on his back and stopped in a mud hole. We took his pack off and got him up, but he refused to move. We were obliged to leave him. We cached the sacks on a rock, tied him to a bush, and left him, thinking to get him later, but we never saw him again. He either got loose and wandered away, or some one found a use for him. I hope he found peace.

There was one large flat-surfaced rock on this part of the trail, canted about forty-five degrees. It was probably ten to twelve feet from the ground to its top edge. There was no other way around. We must force the animals straight up the face of it. At its bottom edge there was a mud puddle about ten feet across and a foot or more deep. We would start the horses on a run some distance from the puddle, then throw them the halter, give them the switch, and, like Ole Olson, they made it in

33

two "yumps." If they got their toes over the top edge on the second jump, they made it. Otherwise they landed in the puddle at the bottom.

I was leading our white pony with three sacks of beans on her back. She didn't quite make the second jump and came straight over backwards, landing on her back on top of the sacks in the mud hole. There she stuck with her four feet in the air. I unbuckled the straps, freeing her from the pack, and got her to her feet. She was now a black pony. I pulled the sacks up out of the mud, but one of them had a large rent in it, and the little white beans sang merrily as they slid out into the mud when I pulled the sack out. We lost about two gallons of beans before I could stop their merry slither. "Drat the beans! Who wants beans anyway!" I said, as I tied up the rent in the sack. And thereby hangs a tale.

By Sunday evening we had been wet four days and had cooked out in the rain. Our clothes, our tent, our bedding were all wet. We had worked wet and slept wet. In fact, we were, by evolutionary process, turning into some kind of amphibians. Our feet, from slipping off sharp rocks and eternally pumping water up and down in our shoes, were not our feet at all. What the outcome would be, should the process go on, was unthinkable.

One day, before we had gotten out of Sheep Camp, where we had been wet for seven days and nights, Harry had come into the tent out of breath, saying,

"A man is going back and has a Yukon stove for sale!"

Duncan had bolted out of the tent, shouting, "Where?" He came back later, dejected. It had been sold.

Monday it was raining a cold rain. The mountains had new snow on their tops. We decided to lay off for the day and rest our feet. Harry discovered another man selling out to go back, and we were lucky enough to buy his Yukon stove for twenty dollars.

They sold at Seattle for seven dollars and fifty cents. But were we glad to get it! We soon had the water out

34

of that tent, and here is where the tale of the beans comes in.

After supper, we were sitting about that wonderful stove, enjoying its warmth, when Harry said, "By gar, I cook some beans. You fellows want some beans?"

"Naw! No beans for us!"

Harry put some on for himself, saying, "I have some tomorrow, by gar!"

The beans came to a boil. He poured the water off, then dropped in a few pieces of bacon and covered them with water again. They were soon plopping away on the hot stove. We got drowsy, and Harry turned in. Duncan followed soon, and I sat dreaming of other things.

The odor from that kettle aroused my curiosity. I got a spoon and quietly dipped out a spoonful of the broth, blew it, and sipped it. All my starving "innards" commenced crying out like a pack of coyotes. I got a tin piepan which we used for a plate, filled it up, beans, soup, meat and all.

As I scraped the last bean from my plate, Duncan made a noise, and I looked at him thinking he was a-sleep. He was grinning and said, "What do you think you are trying to do? Tsk! TSK!"

"You are supposed to be asleep," I said.

He crawled out quietly, got a pan, filled it up, and together we cleaned out the beans. As we were scraping our last pan, Harry stuck his head out of his blankets and said, "Yah, I get beans tomorrow."

This broke us into liking beans, and from then on we could be led up to a feed of beans any time without shying.

Tuesday morning we had just finished breakfast and were thinking to start the day's struggle. I heard a fellow near the tent begging someone to take some burros off his hands as he was through with them. I opened the tent flap and he came forward, leading three fine burros. They were in fine condition, had halters and pack saddles. He begged us to take them, but we said "No." He led them off into the brush, we heard three shots, and that was the end of the burros.

Around Sheep Camp, up to the foot of the pass, between and below, one could hear from one to several shots fired occasionally during the day, ending the miseries of poor horses.

To my knowledge forty or fifty horses had to be shot, from Sheep Camp to the foot of the pass, during our sojourn on that three miles of trail. Probably two hundred lay along the trail from the mouth of the canyon to the foot of the pass. We sometimes were obliged to step on one where it lay in a hole on the trail with a bullet hole in its head. They wore out and starved till they could go no more and lay down. Served their masters faithfully to the last step. It was pitiful.

We got our stuff to Stone House by noon except a load for one horse and a pack on two of our backs. Our second horse went down as we were returning in the forenoon. We were obliged to leave it there for the time, thinking it might be up when we returned. If not, we would shoot it. But some one must have thought we had deserted it, and he put it out of its misery. We were incensed but couldn't blame him much. The poor brute had about reached the end.

I dislike to tell you of these things, but I must be as truthful as possible. We were necessarily cruel, and it pains me about as much thinking about it today as it did while going through the experience. So far as I am concerned, the misery, grief, and pain suffered by man and beast on those trails were greater loss than all the gold of Klondike was gain. I'll be glad when I get beyond the dying and dead horses in this narrative.

Duncan and I, with packs on our backs, went straight through to the foot of the pass. Harry brought along the white pony with a pack. According to my notes, written as I rested my pack on a rock just above Stone House, I had in my pack one sleeping bag, one stove full of wood and oven full of tins, three joints of pipe, one coat, and one ax. "I rest every little ways because of the rough going."

As I neared the pass, a fellow going down the trail said to me, "Cooking as you go, neighbor?" For a few moments, I did not get his meaning, but went right along. It dawned on me finally, and I looked up over my shoulder where the stove was perched on top of the load and saw quite a volume of smoke coming from the pipe hole. I quickly backed up to a rock, resting the pack, unbuckled the straps and found the stove quite hot. The red coals had not all been dumped out, apparently, and the fire box full of wood had ignited. I was startled, thinking the hot bottom might have ruined my sheepskin coat just below, but I had been warned just in time. Later, I saw another fellow going up the trail with smoke pouring from his stove, and I saw how funny it looked. Seemed like he had fired up the boiler to help him navigate.

We reached the foot of the pass finally and beheld a strange camp. The many tents scattered about looked like a strong wind had knocked them every which way. We had left the timber below at Sheep Camp, and even brush was one and a half miles below. Since there were no poles available to support the tents, the whole camp seemed to be on a big spree. Some had oars along which served in a kind of way, but most of the tents were draped over and about the rocks.

After some looking about we found it necessary to make our camp spot among the rocks. Harry had come up and very thoughfully had brought a pole with him. We found a place on the hillside where the crumbled rocks were not so large but were lying in a slide of about forty-five degrees angle. We pulled them down and, leveling them the best we could, stuck the pole at the lower end, hung the tent from it to the rocks above guying it out with rocks.

We had a shelter, but what fun trying to drape our bodies over bags and rocks for the next seven nights.

37

We packed on one pony and on our backs from below, bringing some sticks with us each time for fuel. The
white pony held out fine. She was still fat and sleek, but
Wednesday night we were out of feed. We were worried
about that poor animal. We were considering feeding it
some of our corn meal of which we had plenty.

Just then who should come milling among the crowd
but Mrs. McLean. She and I were glad to meet again. After some talk, I told her of our feed shortage just as a
passing remark. She said, "Come over and meet my husband." I went with her a short ways and stopped before
a man on his knees strapping up his pack. She said,
"John, meet Mr. Medill. This is the young man who helped
me repack the horse down the trail."

He reached up his hand and said, "Glad to meet you,
Mr. Medill." He had a full, quite long beard, and while
it was difficult to say how old he was, I was certain he
was much older than she.

She then turned to me and said, "Get something to
hold them and I'll give you a feed of oats for your horse."
I protested, but she insisted, saying, "I wouldn't do it for
anyone else." and made me bring a sack, into which she
poured a good peck of oats. I never saw the McLeans
again.

Thursday, the sixteenth, like Wednesday, it was raining and snowing, with a couple of inches of snow on the
ground, and we had still another load to bring up. Had
been wet every trip. We seemed to be in the clouds. A
heavy, swirling fog, with the wet snow and rain pene-
trating through or under our oil coats.

As we were about to go down the trail, a worried
looking man came rushing up to ask if we were through
with the pony. "We have one more trip," we said. He
said, "I have just got to get a horse, we are in trouble."
We considered a moment and decided we could bring the
rest of our stuff on our backs by all three bringing a good
load, and we should not have the pain of shooting the
pony. She was not in his affections as in ours. We turned

her over to him, warning him not to shoot her if he could give her to someone else, to which he agreed.

He had just gone down the trail about ten minutes when who should come to me with a pack on his back but the young Indian to whom I had promised the pony at Finnegan's Point.

"Why you geeve my pony away?"

"Well, you hadn't shown up, so I thought you had forgotten it."

"No, I wanted the pony!"

"Well, that man has only today's packing to make, and you can get her from him sometime today, if you watch him." I did not see my young friend again. I sincerely hope he got the pony, for I am sure he would give her good care.

This is the foot of the pass. You don't know how glad I am. We can now take a look back for the first time. Ten days in that awful canyon to come nine miles, and we made good time at that.

VI

CHILKOOT PASS

Friday, the seventeenth, it was too stormy to cross the pass, and we passed the day resting up. Our feet, Duncan's and mine, were in a queer condition. Harry's were all right. The reason for this was to be found in the kind of shoes we had been wearing. Our shoes had thin soles; Harry had heavy-soled shoes. Our feet were not skinned in the least, but every bone in them was as sore as a boil. I had never experienced such a thing before. Seemed like the slipping and bending over the sharp rocks had sprained all the ligaments. Because of the pain occasioned when we stepped on a sharp rock or slipped off one, we had many comical falls. Will tell you of one such later.

As we rested this day, we made a trip down to the brush and brought up a load of firewood, brush of poor quality. We also had time to think of Harry's services which had been so admirable that we then and there made him a third partner in our grub supply.

Now came up to us a report of the flood which had swept away a portion of Sheep Camp. We had escaped by half a day. A lake up in the mountain tops had broken its barriers. Ice and water poured down the valley near Stone House on the same side of the canyon as Sheep Camp. It swept away all tents near the stream at Sheep Camp, taking the life of one man and injuring several others, but not killing one-hundred men, as some reports had it. The next spring a glacier from the opposite side killed sixty-five men.

We had camped seven days on the part of Sheep Camp that was cleaned out. We knew that when the report got outside the papers would be full of the incident. As the folks back home were following us by the letters sent along the trail, when occasion permitted, they would know we were in the danger zone. To allay their fears, we

40

sent a letter down the trail at once, informing them we were safe. They got the letter all right but it was in December!

We were sitting around the stove that evening. The storm had quieted down. A dead calm had fallen over the camp, when all of a sudden a splitting blast from a trumpet rent the air. An unusual thing under the circumstances. Then a voice—

"Is that you, Scottie?"

"Aye, it's me, and I'll gie ye Auld Lang Syne frae the summit, the morn."

Only an impulse of a wandering Scot. But to us who knew something of the history and nature of this indomitable people, it was a defy to the depths and an "Excelsior" to the heights.

You folks, no doubt, think of the Chilkoot Trail and Pass as perpetually covered with snow. Photographers and artists have given that impression. But I am inclined to the belief that, while the snow covered Pass of winter may be more striking, the bare Pass of summer and fall is much more trying to him who climbs.

However that may be, we must go on over the bare Chilkoot Pass. And again this Saturday morning the wind and rain are back with us after the calm of the evening before. The clouds hang down one-third of the way from the top of the Pass. We each take a fifty pound sack for a start, expecting difficulties that a heavier pack would aggravate. We climb up into the clouds where the visibility is limited to a few rods at most.

As we reached that notch in the mountain rim, the Pass, the roaring wind nearly took us off our feet! It was impossible to speak to each other even though we shouted. By watching the slippery rocks as we passed through and down the other side, we could follow the trail by the scarified tops of the rocks, made so by many nailed shoes having passed that way. We went on down nearly a quarter of a mile, when we heard the waves lapping on the shores of Crater Lake. Though but fifty yards away, we

41

could not see the lake. Selecting a large flat rock on the right side of the trail, we cached our packs and covered them with a canvas we had brought for a sail on our future boat.

It was like working in the dark, and we got wet, good and plenty. We made two trips over in the afternoon. Wet each time, but we felt fine in the evening. Sunday we made two trips by noon. Got wet each time, as usual. At noon, the sky cleared, and as we went over the top, we got a wonderful view and came back dry for the first time.

When we awoke Monday morning, it was snowing and raining, turnabout. We went over the top, however, and found four inches of snow! Made two trips before noon, and I laid up that afternoon, as I was not feeling so well, but the others went over twice. Tuesday, raining as usual. By noon, it cleared up and the sun came out. We got all over but one pack, and I went back for it.

As I went down the Pass, I passed two men and two women, about two-thirds up. They had been there when I had gone over the last trip. Detaining them were two horses they were trying to lead over the Pass by zigzagging across the hillside. They had finally gotten out on a ledge, where one of the horses spread out his legs in terror and couldn't be budged. The high position was too much for him. He was paralyzed with fear. I had gone down about one hundred yards below them when I heard a shot. I looked up in time to see that poor beast rear up on his hind legs and go over the cliff backwards, falling about one hundred feet, with a squash. They were gone when I returned, so I suppose they got the other horse over.

I had seen, a few days before, some men try to get a large ox over, but he stopped only a third of the way up and had to be shot. Apparently some horses had been taken over, for I found dead ones scattered along the trail between Crater and Long Lakes.

We saw several women hanging to the arms of their men folks. The men had packs and clung to the rocks while the women clung to the men. These women had taken to overalls to make the ascent, which was the sensible thing to do.

As I reached about the middle of the Pass on my last trip, I rested my pack on a rock, took out my note book, and wrote a farewell to the Pass and all below. As I looked down, the horrible sight of many dead horses drew my attention more than the beauty of the landscape.

There were three large blocks of rock, about the size of one-story houses forming a triangle at the bottom of the Pass, off to one side. I could distinctly see a mass of dead horses lying in that enclosure where they had been led and shot. I could clearly make out nine, but many more were around the foot of the Pass.

I sadly rose with my burden and went on up over the top for the last time. As I stumbled down to the lake, I was surprised to find a ferry-boat waiting my arrival. The boys had all our stuff aboard and were waiting for my pack. It costs us two cents per pound but saved us time and much hard labor. We were fortunate to find the boatmen at a dull spell in business. Usually, we learned, one had considerable waiting to do. Those boatmen were reaping a harvest. On that one load they had over one hundred dollars freight.

The lake is two miles long, the fountain-head of the Yukon river; and, if you stay with me long enough, I'll take you twenty-four hundred miles to its mouth in the Bering Sea.

We walked around the lake and reached the far end about the time the boat did. Caching our goods on a big rock and covering them with the sail, we took a camp outfit in our pack-straps and struck out down the outlet to Long Lake, three and one-half miles away.

We had to cross and recross the stream a number of times. It was not over knee-deep, but deep enough to fill our shoes. A short ways below Crater Lake, the scar in the rock through which the stream travels, was filled with a small glacier, some three hundred to four hundred yards long. The stream flowed underneath, and we traveled over the top.

This three and one-half miles to Long Lake wasn't so bad. Fairly level, and altogether agreeable, except where we waded the stream and got our feet wet. Long Lake is one and one-half miles long, one of many lakes in the Yukon river that are like beads on a string. There we found some timber again and soon had a comfortable camp set up.

Wednesday morning, the twenty-second, we began packing from Crater Lake. It was raining, sleeting, blowing and cold; dead horses were here and there. One poor little burro kicking his last from starvation hadn't been relieved by a shot.

In the midst of tragedy, there is always some comedy if we can only see it. Before we left home, we were some kind of lower strata gentlemen. On the trail, when we were nicely messed up, one of use would say to the other with a grin, "If they could only see us now!" This would bring a laugh and cheer us up a little, which we sorely needed at times.

I was slopping along from Crater Lake with two sacks of corn meal in my pack-straps, which weighed something more than one hundred pounds because of the amount of water they had soaked up. As I crossed the stream in about one-and-a-half feet of water, I stepped on a round, slippery stone. My foot slipped off, and every bone in my foot cried out in pain—the sore bones still being with us. Impelled by the weight of the sacks on the back of my neck, I dove head first into the sand and gravel on the bottom of the stream. No chance to raise my head above water as the sacks held it down. Finding I couldn't rise that way, there was only one thing to do. I rolled over on my back, sacks going down and my head coming up so that I got a breath of air. I worked myself

44

into a sitting position. Looking about and seeing no one in sight, I remarked to myself, "If they could only see me now!"

Returning with our packs the second day, we observed a crowd of people at the foot of the hill at this end of Long Lake. We inquired the cause of all the gathering and were told they were burying a man who had died the night before. The poor fellow had found his Klondike after the worst of the trail had been covered. My thoughts went to his folks back home.

By this time some of our goods were getting quite wet. Each sack of flour, meal, or what-not had, on the outside, an extra heavy canvas seamless sack. These extra outside sacks were guaranteed water proof, but of course the water penetrated. The corn meal, of which we had five hundred pounds, was very wet. The water penetrated the meal, but flour is different. Water penetrates flour about one fourth inch, which forms dough. This dough, being plastic, gives with the movements of the sack, protecting all the inside flour. This dough sticks to the sack, and the inside flour can be removed any time. We lost nothing but corn meal, and not all we had of that. We took it along as it was and saw the time when musty corn meal was better than starvation.

While we were camped at Long Lake, a woman with an escort and four tons of outfit passed. She seemed to have money enough to rush right along and was doing it. I helped to load, on the ferry there, the goods of a show troupe of five girls bound for Dawson. Their goods were done up in sealed zinc cubical containers, sixteen inches on the edge.

After slopping back and forth, we got all of our goods down to Long Lake by Friday night. The weather cleared in the afternoon.

Saturday morning, when we looked out, there was eight inches of snow, and it was coming down in great wet flakes. We decided to rest up for the day, but soon heard some one shouting outside. There before our tent was the ferry-boat. The ferry-man told us to come on; this was our best chance, if we waited for good weather our competition for the boat would be fierce. Duncan jumped up saying, "Let's go!" In half an hour, our stuff was going across the lake, and we were jumping the rocks around the shore. It was tough! Cold, wet snow, rocks, and mud!

We piled our goods on a rock, wet and muddy and covered them. Then, taking heavy c a m p packs, we started around Deep Lake for Lake Linderman, three miles away over a muddy, rough trail. When we finally came to the ridge overlooking Linderman, away down there one and a half miles below, we got a thrill. The sun was shining down there. No snow, and a big camp on the lakeside looked too comfortable to be real—a real fairy land.

Like thirsty cattle in a desert, at sight of water we hurried down the mountain. When we reached Linderman, we found it to be as wonderfully comfortable as it looked. Some outfit had just pulled out leaving a fine dry camp spot near the w a t e r. They had had their tent ground covered with a deep bed of curly shavings, and on this spot, we pitched our tent and were happy. That was grand! We were soon dry, had lots of dry wood, lots of good cooking, and we felt like millionaires.

VII

LAKE LINDERMAN

That was surely a busy camp. Saws and hammers going all day long, and such a sweet smell of new pine wood. Harry made some fine bread. We cooked up some stuff in advance and got ready to bring our goods from Long Lake. By ferrying over Deep Lake, which is one-half mile long, and packing steadily, we landed everything at Linderman on Tuesday, and our last big packing was done—what a relief!

Wednesday, we spent going among the busy bees, learning all we could—where to get logs, how whipsawing was done. We saw ten or twelve boats pull away down the Lake during the day, heading for the Yukon River. Every day a number were ready and pulled out.

Linderman is four miles long, and is in the form of a right-angle, two miles to the right and two miles to the left around the point of a mountain. Its setting is extremely beautiful, surrounded by snow clad mountain peaks. Timber, a kind of spruce, I believe, covers the mountain sides up into the snows. The peaks are bare except for snow.

Thursday, the thirtieth of September, was a beautiful sunny day; and we went about a mile back along the mountain side to begin our whip-sawing of boards for our boat. We found a horse for the purpose already up, and we took possession. This horse for whip-sawing is made by placing two logs, about eight to twelve inches thick, eight feet above the ground on supports, trees, legs, or such. By leaning two skid logs against these, the logs to be whip-sawed can be rolled or skidded up onto the horse.

We felled a tree about fourteen inches at the butt, and after facing it on two sides twenty feet with the ax, we sawed it off and skidded it up onto the horse or horse-logs. We then lined it on the surfaced sides three-fourths of an inch between the lines, as we wanted to cut boards

47

that thick. Cord and blue chalk had been brought from Seattle for that purpose, along with pitch, nails, oakum, and other necessaries for boat construction.

With one man below and one on top, one on each end of the saw, it was a pull down, pull up affair. By night, we had five nice boards twenty feet long. I left for camp before they were finished, to prepare supper, and the other boys brought the boards. We felt good now that we knew we could cut the boards necessary for the job. But next morning we got another jolt. We looked out on ten inches of snow, and snow falling like sixty. It was no time to loaf by the way-side. We struck out for the timber, taking a couple of short pieces of rope along.

We got our log up on the horse, but we could neither line the log decently nor see the lines afterwards for the falling soft snow. In desperation, we sawed the log by guess, and I'll warrant no such boards were ever sawed before. They ran all the way from one-half to two and one-half inches thick. We consoled ourselves by saying, "We can plane them down." We drew five more boards to camp that night on the top of the snow. Snow was good for that at least.

It froze hard Friday night, and Saturday morning the air was calm. We worked all day on the boat and got quite a little done. But when we tried to plane the bumps off the boards of different thicknesses, our plane choked up with the green sappy shavings. We tried a sharp ax, but that was unsatisfactory also. We thought for awhile it would be necessary to go back and saw some more boards. We finally decided to make the bottom with the even-thickness boards, then place the uneven on the sides, heavy board against heavy, and light against light. We did this, and clinched every nail.

By Thursday night, we had it calked, pitched, and trimmed. A fairly nice looking cat boat, eighteen feet long, two feet deep, with four and a half foot beam, and a mast fitted in the beam. Friday morning was a nice morning after snow, rain, and shine, for working on the boat. It had taken us eight days, and this Friday was October the seventh.

We launched the boat. It rode an even keel and didn't leak. "Hurrah! !" We loaded up in a hurry after noon and were off down the lake. Getting a little wind, we pulled up the sail, and everything was fine for a while. Then the wind rose, as we rounded the point, and it got so strong we had to lower the sail and take the oars. The wind got to be quite a squall, as we approached the north end of the lake, and the waves were slashing up on the shore and slamming back in a mean manner. It was shallow water, and we were suddenly placed in an uncomfortable position. The water was full of round boulders, from a foot to six or ten feet across. How to dodge those rocks with the wind driving us on to them! We got by till about three boat lengths off shore when a receding wave set us down squarely on top of a large boulder about four feet across. It caught the boat about a third of its length from the prow. The next wave pounded us, and another. The boys tried to push off by putting their oars on the bottom, but we were solidly anchored on top of that rock. All we could do was swing a little this way or that. Duncan finally went over the prow up to his thighs, got his back under the prow, and, with the help of the next wave, slid the boat off the rock, then guided it to shore where we others jumped out and lent a hand, running it up as far as possible.

This accident seemed a small affair, but it cost us several days' time. The boat, with its heavy load swinging on that rock, was sprung, necessitating a drying and recalking before we could go on. This we did at the head of Bennett Lake.

We unloaded the boat there at the foot of Linderman and made camp. We found the boat was leaking. Saturday, we shifted camp to the head of Bennett, as we must portage between these lakes. The connecting stream is only three-fourths mile long, but it is one continuous cascade through a narrow rocky bed. Sunday, we let the boat carefully down this channel by walking on the rocks on shore, holding the rope, and protecting the boat from striking against the shore rocks by keeping it off with an oar, two of us walking opposite the boat with oars for the purpose. When we got to Lake Bennett, we pulled it on shore and turned it over to dry.

Here, on Bennett, where the Skagway trail came in, we found about thirty tents and everybody busy. On the south side of the portage between these lakes, as we packed our goods over, we passed the grave of a Klondiker who was reported to have committed suicide after losing his outfit in the connecting stream. Four stakes connected by four poles enclosed the grave and on a little piece of board, nailed to one of the stakes, was roughly inscribed, "J. W. Mathers."

Tuesday morning, while we were finishing the packing from the foot of lake Linderman, Duncan stayed at camp and recalked and pitched the boat bottom. Having everything ready after dinner we loaded up and pulled down Lake Bennett, about half way. Just below the island on the right hand bank, among the trees, we camped. Lake Bennett is listed as twenty-six miles long. We were very weary after our long pull, and I was ill and weak, continuing so a greater part of the run to Dawson. It was well for me that we were in the boat instead of on the Pass. Of course, we had little ups and downs in health; the wonder was that we did not all die. Everything considered, we kept in remarkable health on the trip.

We covered the remainder of Bennett and the connecting stream, Caribou Crossing, by Wednesday night, and camped on the head of Lake Tagish or Takou. This lake is nineteen miles long and has two inlets on the right hand side, the Big and Little Windy arms. We crossed Lake Tagish Thursday and camped at its foot. The next morning, while running the five-mile connection stream between that lake and Lake Marsh, we came suddenly upon the British flag, planted on the right hand side of the stream. Mounties waved us in, and we found the

Canadian Customs House, a few log cabins, which had just been established. They kept us several hours. They didn't seem to be in any hurry. We finally learned that the non-uniformed man walking about outside (we were not in any office) was the customs officer. We asked him what he wanted of us.

"We have to collect duty on your outfit. How much have you got?"

"A two-man outfit," we answered.

"How much money have you?"

Thinking truth the better policy, we told him we had just forty-two dollars left. What do you think he said?

"That will be all right."

"But," we protested, "You wouldn't take a man's last dollar?"

"You'll not need any money at Dawson. The hills are full of gold."

We gave him our last dollar, and he wrote us the following receipt on a scrap of paper.

"Medill Bros. have paid duty on their outfit."

No signature, no amount stated, just that! They let us go. We were stunned. But we were in a foreign country and glad to leave its officers at the first contact.

Just as we were about to embark, a dugout canoe loaded with Indians came down the river, and tacked to the top of their mast was a large American flag. The Mounties waved for them to come in. The Indians professed ignorance and continued to drift by. The Mounties, seeing they couldn't get the Indians in, yelled at them, "Take that flag down!" The Indians yelled back, "No, this heap good flag!" The Mounties turned away with a grin, which closed the incident.

Later, down in the diggings, we met three friends with whom we had become acquainted on the trail. One was an ex-Jack Tar, another was an ex-British sailor. They both had the British dialect strong. We asked what the customs officer charged them on their very complete, three-man outfit. They told us he charged them twenty dollars.

In the last few years, I have heard that the Canadian Government punished the early customs officials for irregularities. I only hope they punished severely enough.

We ran on down to Lake Marsh, and there got a wind from behind. We ran up the sail, and by using the oars also, we went kiting along. In fact, toward the foot of the lake, we were kiting too much. The wind grew and grew, and the waves rose till they were breaking over the boat sides. The shore was rocky along there or we would have run in for safety. But coming to a low swampy shore, we did run in near the foot of the lake and camped on the spongy moss. We had to go back a way among some willows before we got ground solid enough to feel comfortable.

Where we turned in to the shore, there was a large rock jutting out from the shore, perhaps one hundred feet, and sticking up from a crevice in the rock was a pole with a white cloth tacked to its top. Very early next morning we heard shouts, and looking out, we saw a boat with several men in it. They wanted to know if they could do anything for us. We assured them there was nothing wrong with us. They said, "We saw your flag of distress there on the rock and thought you were having trouble." "No," we said, "that was there before we came." We thanked them for stopping and they went on.

Saturday, the sixteenth, we left the Lake early, hoping we might reach Miles Canyon that day. The swift current also encouraged us to think this, as we sped down the connecting stream between Marsh and Labarge. It was just as well, night coming on, that we were obliged to camp without reaching the canyon, for it is not too safe a place to run upon suddenly.

The next morning we had been running along for about half an hour, the river narrowing and the current gaining speed, when suddenly a red flag, fluttering from a stick on the bank, halted our oars. Nailed to a tree, was a small board from which the word "CANNON" seemed to scream at us and made our nerves tingle. We set ourselves for action, for we were being swept along at a good pace and didn't want to plump into the canyon without time to "confess our sins." Flying around a sharp bend to the left—"What now!" "What the Sam Hill!"

Our river had terminated against the side of the mountain.

VIII

MILES CANYON

Voices on the right brought our attention that way. "Pull in here!" they shouted. There was an elbow in the right bank, almost still water, and the land sloped up gently to a grassy bench. On this bench were a number of men and a quantity of supplies. We pulled in there quicker than I can write it, you may guess. We landed and made the boat fast to a tree. Then we looked to where the stream had vanished against the side of the mountain. For a minute we could not understand where that big stream had gone, but, gazing steadily into the gloom over there, we finally made out what seemed like a slit in the rock formation at the far right-hand corner. Closer observation disclosed a kind of sluing of the pent-up waters into the slit, and that was the entrance to Miles Canyon.

From our point on shore, we were looking across the canyon's mouth, which made it difficult to see. The perpendicular rock wall on this side of the mouth was about thirty feet high, and it seemed to blend with the higher rock wall beyond, which ran away up into a mountain that seemed to lean away back to the sky. The mountain side was covered with pine above the sheer rock abutment.

"So this is Miles Canyon!" we queried, rather talking to ourselves than those present. We had read about it, had it pictured in our minds, but, like most preconceptions, it was extravagantly different. It is worth seeing, that threatening, silent slit in the rock wall, from back in the elbow on the right bank. No other part of the canyon made such an impression on my mind.

The depth of the water we could only surmise. A large, broad river had narrowed to about thirty feet to go through that slit in the rock. And how quietly it slid in! But no sooner had it entered than it began to roar, and

54

only down in that canyon in a boat does one get the full force of the roar, or find the full fury of the current.

The walls of the canyon are made up of hexagonal perpendicular columns of black rock, about three feet, perhaps, on each edge of the hexagons, but the upright shafts go down out of sight. They are all welded together in a solid body, forming a very unique wall.

We had promised, faithfully, before leaving home, "You don't need to worry about us running Miles Canyon, we will build a boat light enough to be portaged." Ahem! We lie and the women like it, but we didn't lie in this case. We had fully intended to portage, but, on looking the situation over, it seemed best to go through.

We walked up on top of the canyon wall and looked down. We walked the full length of the canyon, three-fourths mile, and looked down. The walls got a little higher as we went down along, perhaps fifty feet. The far wall on the mountain side was higher. On our side the land went back quite a way fairly level, and we had a good place to walk along and study the barrier to our progress.

The height, width, and current of this canyon varies with the person looking at it; I am giving simply my own impressions.

Down about two-thirds the length, there was, on the far side, a large, half-circular notch in the wall where the Canyon widened out. The notch extended about fifty yards along the wall, I would say. The walls of this notch were perpendicular and of the same formation as the rest. But the far wall was much higher than the rest, from having encroached on the mountain side. In this notch was a large whirlpool, and, as we looked, a pine tree came down the canyon. It was still green and was coming top first. It was probably seventy-five feet long and a foot thick at the butt. We watched with interest as it swung over into the whirlpool. It went slowly around the pool, getting closer to the center. As the top reached the center, it went under the water. Then the trunk went gradually under the water, and finally, as it was drawn down, the roots shot up into the air ten or twelve feet, the tree actually going down head first and disappearing. So far as we know, it is still going down.

We examined the canyon to its outlet. At its outlet there was an eddy that swirled to the right bank around the corner of the high perpendicular wall. The shore here sloped back sensibly and made not a bad place to land, but one must pull quickly to the right, when shot from the canyon, else he would be carried past the eddy and go on down the current.

Miles Canyon was said to be three-fourths of a mile long, and drift wood passed through it in two minutes, about twenty-two and one-half miles per hour.

We examined every thing carefully as we returned up the wall. We decided the current was not too bad but we didn't realize that looking down on the current from above was much different from looking at it at water level. Being held back by the side walls the water combs up in the middle and forms great up-and-down shoots on the comb. We could not appraise those shoots from the top of the wall. By avoiding the big whirlpool and making a quick right turn at the outlet, we felt the canyon could be run safely with our small boat.

Going back up to the Canyon head, we were just in time, we thought, and still think, to save the life of one, if not two Mounties—fine, intelligent-looking, young men. One was on top of the wall holding a rope attached to a light canoe down at the foot of the wall, the other, in the canoe working it out by a paddle to the slit in the wall. We asked them what they were trying to do. They were going to let the canoe down, one holding it by the rope on top of the wall, the other in the canoe to keep if off the wall with the paddle.

We asked them if they had ever done it before. They said they hadn't We argued it couldn't be done without catastrophe; that when the current got hold of the canoe, it would either swamp it, throwing the man below into the water, or pull the man above off the cliff into the canyon, and likely both things would happen, for the man above had the rope tied about his middle!

We also pointed out that the canoe was light and could easily be carried over the portage, which was good. We assured them if our boat were so light, we would never think of running through, we would portage. We had to beg those fellows not to try it, before we got them to desist. The canoe would, perhaps, have carried them safely through, had they got in together and turned it loose, using their paddles to keep it straight. But their plan would have been disastrous.

If a man were a good swimmer and were not overcome by the icy waters, I see no reason why he could not swim the canyon. Those men said they could not swim.

Brother and I were good swimmers, and our only fear, should we be wrecked running through, was what would the icy water do to us. Of course we would lose our outfit.

We got back to our boat fully determined to shoot the canyon. We threw out on the bank a camp outfit, and enough provisions to keep us a while in the event we were wrecked and lived through it. We shed all our clothing but shirt, overalls and socks. Harry and Duncan took the oars and I, the sweep. We rowed slowly over to the slit in the wall. When we got before the slit, the current took us gently, lovingly, into its arms and drew us in.

At the entrance, the water sang a low sweet song against the sides, but, like Ulysses strapped to the mast, we could not stay. The siren sang, but we were as effectively bound as Ulysses. It seemed to us on that smooth intake, we could drift forever. But zounds! An upshot hit us under the prow! The prow heaved up in the air! The boat quivered and rolled, and before we could catch our breath, we pitched down into the back of the next upshot, only to be heaved higher.

I never rode a bucking bronco, but our boat seemed bent on excelling the wildest bronc.

The roar grew deafening. Boom! Up she went! Down she pitched! Boom! Another upshot under the prow! Boom! Boom! Boom! Up, down! Up, down! Rolling this way and that! Waters hissed and roared like all the devils let loose! We were nearing the big whirlpool notch. Our prow was being boomed up faster than it could come down. Three upshots hit under the prow in succession, and up she went at about a forty-five degree angle and swung toward the left wall. The next upshot behind hit me on the back of the neck and swashed by me into the boat. I yelled, "Blankety, blank, we're going down!" What the others yelled, if anything, I don't know. I do know they didn't hear me for the roar. Slam! Down came the fore part on the water, before I had time to get out all of my exclamation.

The boys' oars hit the water just at the moment and straightened us with the current.

Only once in a while could they touch the water with the oars. The last touch was a valuable one. We were off! Plunging up and down! Rolling and quivering! Flying past the big whirlpool and out the mouth of the Canyon!

We shot out of the mouth so swiftly we came near going past the eddy. A few hard pulls brought us over, and the next moment we were on shore and the boat was looking as quiet and innocent as the cat after swallowing the canary.

"Whew. An inch is as good as a mile, boys! Let's pack!"

IX

WHITE HORSE RAPIDS

Sunday, October 17, we had cleared the C a n y o n, packed over our camp outfit, shoved off, and headed for White Horse Rapids.

A short ways below the Canyon the stream widens out considerably and is full of black rounded boulders showing below and above the water, the water being shallower because of greater width. We had to be wary not to hit any of these boulders as we were carried swiftly along by the current. About three miles below Miles Canyon, we sighted White Horse Rapids ahead about half a mile, and we pulled to shore on the left bank. Where we pulled in happened to be the beginning of the portage for the Rapids. A good trail led from there down along the top of a rock wall to the Rapids, about half a mile.

We tied up there at the beginning of the portage and went down to examine the White Horse. White Horse it was indeed! For about a half mile above, the stream was about two hundred or more yards wide, with rock walls perhaps twenty feet high, a wide canyon with low walls. These walls, down at the Rapids, came out to meet each other. At one time, no doubt, they did meet, forming a falls. But the water, carrying its sand, gravel and ice, had cut through, leaving a narrow gap through which the water spurted for a length of nearly one hundred feet. And such a spout! The water flew ten, fifteen feet into the air, white foam with a cloud of spray above it all.

These rock arms, which ran out from either shore, had been worn down from their original height at the shore walls till they slanted gradually into the water at the spout. The water lapped up over this slanting arm on our side where we figured we could ease the boat over, if it were empty.

We stayed there awhile to see s e v e r a l boats go through, large twenty-four and thirty-foot boats. It was a sight. Those men knew their business.

By the way, here is where W. P. Gates got his sobriquet, "Swiftwater Bill." We met him later. He remained here for a time, piloting boats through the Canyon and White Horse.

Up the river, there came a boat around the bend, four men at the oars and one standing up in the stern with a long sweep end under his arm, and holding that end for dear life! As the boat nears us, we see it is canvassed from the prow to the mast. The canvas is stretched over a pole running from the prow to the mast, and is tacked to the boat sides, making a sloping deck to shed the water both ways—they need it. The oarsmen increase their p o w e r gradually as they near the Spout; then, throwing every ounce of their strength into it, the helmsman crouches forward, his eyes riveted on the center of the spout! Bang! They hit the Spout in the center and are lost to view for one, two, three, four seconds or more they are out of sight—we are uneasy—then like a huge porpoise, the boat shoots out the side of the spray to the left and comes to a stop in the large eddy behind the rock arm—all and everything dripping water. Believe me, it was a great dive.

Possibly, following the ice down in the spring, when the water may be much higher, this Spout may not be so formidable. It may smooth out considerably, as the rock arms are covered higher up. However that may be, I have tried to describe it as we found it in October, 1897. It may change, as change it must, when those arms are cut away.

We turned away to go back to our boat up the stream. One of us exclaimed, "We can run it!" The other said nothing. I looked at them a moment and said, "Well, boys, there is the boat up yonder, you can run it if you choose, but I will not go with you. The Canyon was bad enough, but this is something else again. Our boat is too small to shoot this successfully—maybe so, maybe not." That settled it.

Shortly before we got to White Horse, an ex-sheriff or deputy sheriff of Seattle, with his company, lost everything but their lives shooting the Spout. They went up on the bank and started a fire to dry out. This ex-officer sat beside the fire drying his gun which he had carried on his person during his swim. The others were getting some wood when they heard a shot. On returning to the fire they found him dead. The report did not disclose whether it was suicide or accident.

Just below the Spout, there was a sand-bar piled up in the center of the stream. Lying crosswise of its upper end, turned over on its side, was a new twenty-five or thirty foot boat. About ten feet of its forward end was gone. It looked as though some one had hacked it off with a dull ax. How it happened, to whom it belonged, what became of its crew, we couldn't learn.

We camped for the night at the upper end of the portage. Monday, we let the boat, empty, down along the wall by the rope, slid it over the sloping arm in about six inches of water, and into the eddy below. We then portaged our stuff, loaded up, and were half way to Lake Labarge, thirty-six miles, by night.

Tuesday, with a good current, we reached Labarge where we got a good breeze behind, and whooped it up half way down the lake, when darkness and rough water drove us to camp.

Here, Tuesday, October nineteenth, on Labarge, and more than half the trip still ahead. But as we left the lake Wednesday morning, we found a fine current, had a wind with us, and made sixty miles by night. We had fine going and good camps for several days.

When we passed the mouth of Big Salmon river, we met the ice flow coming out of it, and the weather turned cold. We had left rain, snow, and wind at the head of Bennett, and had had fine weather till now, but now we were in for something different. Next morning, we had four inches of snow, and still snowing. It stopped after awhile but remained cold, below freezing, a little.

Running along swiftly, we came to a little Indian village on the right bank. We let the boat slide in along the shore and looked down at it. Down to the shore, came a horde of natives. What a sight! Mostly children, from toddlers to young men and women. Several of the youngest hadn't a stitch of clothing on; some, older, in their bare feet in the snow. The still older ones had moccasins and all kinds of rags. They were all shouting, "Breed! Breed!" We made out finally that they wanted bread. They must have gotten the pronunciation of that word from Scots in the service of the Hudson Bay Company.

We considered a moment and thought of some flapjacks left over from breakfast and turned the boat to land. Immediately, the boat was over-run by young imps. All had change in their hands, and each wanted to be the first to buy "Breed." Harry got out the grub-box and pulled out six cakes.

"How much?" they cried in unison, holding out their hands full of change and grabbing for the cakes.

"Half a dollar." He passed them to one, taking the half-dollar. He pulled out some more and sold those. "That's all," he said.

I had made some corn cake away back up the trail some where, after our baking powder had played out. It was made in a bread pan about six by ten inches and was about three-fourths inch thick. It was beautifully yellow, but as hard as nails. I figured on softening it up some day, but we couldn't eat it the way it was.

Harry, feeling around, at their insistence, pulled out this cake. There was a great clamor. One young fellow grabbed it and passed Harry half a dollar. He then jumped ashore, took a corner of that cake in his teeth, failed to bite off any, then handed it back to Harry, saying, "Half dol!" Harry gave him the money and took the cake. Then he shooed them off the boat, or tried to. A young women reached out to Harry, saying, "Breed, breed," pointing to where he had thrown the cake. He gave her the cake and took her half dollar. She jumped on the shore with a look of success on her face, and the cake in her hand. She turned around, facing us, put a corner of the cake in her mouth trying to bite a piece off as the young fellow had tried but could not do it. The crowd gave her the laugh and said many things we did not understand, but she shook her head and tucked the cake up under her arm, with a shrug. She knew what to do with that cake.

We had a time getting them off the boat and decided, "Never again!" We had just pushed off and were drifting, when a young man came down to the shore, holding out a five dollar gold piece in his open hand, and saying, "Medcin, Medcin!" We finally understood, he wanted medicine.

"What is the matter with you?" Duncan asked.

"Poor Sy seek, Poor Sy seek."

"Where are you sick?" He caught his hand to his throat.

We shook our heads, but he followed us quite a way.

A day or two later, we came to a little camp on the left bank. We thought it was McCormac's Post, a few log cabins and some tents. We needed some little things and Harry ran up to get them. Duncan stood on shore holding the boat's rope. Down over the bank, came an old squaw, holding, spread out, a nice, large, red, sun dried salmon.

"Buy salmon?" she queried.

"No!" Duncan replied.

"How much?" I asked.

"Two dollars."

Harry had passed me a Canadian two dollar bill after his sales the other day, and as I had seen sun-dried salmon before, and wondered what it might be like, I passed the bill over and took the fish. She went away, and soon a tall, thin young woman, a breed, came down over the bank. She had on a calico dress of faded color. It fitted her like a long narrow sack, with a draw string at the neck. She had some kind of black dried meat under her arm and her two hands under the opposite elbows for warmth. She sidled up to Duncan—both about six feet tall. He wouldn't look at her. She said,

"Buy some bear meat?"

"Haven't any money."

"Give me chew tobacco," bumping him with an elbow.

"Haven't any tobacco."

"Yes, you have. I see it in your pocket!" Duncan shrugged. Harry came back, and we pulled out.

The next morning there was eight to ten inches of snow, and more ice floating on the river. We were in a desperate hurry. About two hundred and fifty miles from Dawson, with conditions getting bad, we suddenly ran into a new experience.

X

WE MEET SWIFTWATER BILL

About midday, October twenty-third and about ten miles above Five-finger Rapids, the shores were blanketed with ten inches of snow, and we had some ice drifting in the river. We were making great speed in the swift current. The boys were helping by lustily applying the oars, while I was on the sweep. There were several boats ahead and several more behind in sight, making all haste possible.

Down ahead on the left bank, we could make out a man standing on a projection of the shore. He had a gun resting in the elbow of his left arm. As we approached, he called out,

"Hello, you fellows!"

"Hello," we called back.

"Say," he said, "if some of you fellows don't stop, there are two men here going to starve to death."

"Why is that?"

"We are on the way out overland from Dawson, and we are out of grub. We have been trying for several days to get some one to stop, but so far have failed, and it's getting serious with us. Some of you boys must relieve us or we are going to starve."

This was all said very hurriedly, as the current carried us along, with oars poised.

"Let's run in and see how they are fixed," one of us said. I swung the sweep, the others plied the oars, and we landed.

The man said, "We can pay you well for any grub you can spare us."

"Well, we have only a two-man outfit for three of us and can't really afford to part with any of it. Some of these boats with a full supply should fix you up."

"Yes, that's true, but we have failed to get any one

65

to stop till you did. Come on up to the camp and meet my pardner."

We went up over the bank to a fire among the trees. There was no tent. We asked them how they managed without a tent. They smiled and said they had a Yukon tent, rabbit skin sleeping bags—new to us.

As the man poking at the fire arose, we noticed he was short and bow-legged, and had a full set of whiskers about two months old. Our first man said to us, "Meet Mr. Gates, better known as Swiftwater Bill."

We said, as we shook hands, "Our names are Medill and Reese."

Swiftwater said, "Well, boys, that's our supply of grub," pointing to a five pound lard pail supported by a stick over the fire. We looked in the pail and it was about one-third full of rice. He said further, "You can name your price for any grub you can spare us, and we will pay you now or give you an order on Dawson."

"Well, as we said before, we are short, and grub is life in this country; but we can't see you starve. We"ll give you a hand-out."

Swiftwater went back among the trees where we could see him kicking the snow about at the root of a tree. He came forward with a fifty pound seamless sack in his hands. He pulled from it another similar sack, and, shaking it, spread it on the snow, saying, "I just want to show you we can pay for the grub." He reached into the first sack again and pulled out what we learned later was a fifteen thousand dollar gold sack. A buckskin sack that holds fifteen thousand dollars worth of gold. And it was heavy! He opened the sack and pulled out gold. Yes! And such a piece! There was no mistaking it. It was gold. The first native gold we had ever seen. He passed it into our hands to heft. It was the shape of a wedge, three to four inches long, two to three inches wide, and one to one-and-a-half inches thick at the butt. We asked him what it was worth, and he said, "Three hundred and eighty-three dollars."

66

He then pulled another smaller sack from the larger one and poured out on the spread sack a handful of nuggets the size of black walnuts with the hulls off. Then another small sack with a handful of nuggets half the size. Another handful of smaller nuggets from another small sack. Then about the same quantity of coarse gold dust from another small sack; and lastly, the same quantity of fine gold from a smaller sack—six quantities in all. He had them arranged in heaps across the big spread sack, with the big nugget at the end, growing finer down the line.

We asked him what he had altogether and he said, "About nine thousand dollars." Then went on, "This is only a few samples I'm taking along."

Naturally, we were impressed. For the first time, we felt our trip might not be in vain. The lurid accounts in the press back home might have had some basis. Our hopes rose.

"Well, boys," said Swiftwater, "You see we can pay you for a hand-out. Do we get it?"

"We'll see what we can do for you, but we don't want your gold."

He filled up his sacks again and returned them to his cache by the tree. While doing this, his partner said to us, "Swiftwater sent out one hundred and sixty thousand dollars on the last out-going boat from Dawson."

"Why didn't you fellows go with the boat?"

"We didn't know we were going till after the boat was gone."

Swiftwater returned and we went down to our boat. He said, "How much grub can we have?"

"You say what you want, and we'll see about letting you have it."

"Well, let's see, can we have a sack of flour?"

We threw out the flour; and, one after the other as he named them, we threw them out; slab of bacon, sack of corn meal, half-sack of chipped potatoes, oat meal, milk, salt, sugar, and other lesser things.

He drew a note book from his pocket and began making a list of the stuff, saying, "How much for this and that?"

"Nothing at all, so far as we know, we may not be able to buy anything at Dawson."

"Yes," he said, "You can still buy some things."

"Well, forget it."

He wouldn't have that, and he wrote out an order payable at Dawson, but he couldn't fill in values received not knowing what they were. He wrote another, in which he said,

"Harry Winters, claim No. 13, Eldorado Creek, give the bearers, Medill Bros., what they want."

W. P. Gates."

Just as impulsive as those big plungers are and just as reckless. That order took in quite a bit of territory considering the property over which Winters had charge. But he seemed to have a hunch we wouldn't ask for all his loose belongings.

Then he wrote another note.

"Alec McDonald,
    Dawson, Y. T.

Dear Mac. Anything you can do for the bearers, Medill Bros., I will consider it a favor.

W. P. Gates."

As he handed this to us, he said, "I don't give a damn if it's fifty thousand dollars I won't owe him anything. And when I come back in the spring, if you boys haven't struck it, come to see me."

With our hopes much raised, and handing them a letter to be mailed at Seattle, we shoved off.

There are several phases of this incident for which we must wait, but the one question uppermost in our minds, just now, was, why did those men miss the last boat out and then start afoot overland seven hundred and fifty miles in winter weather?

68

I''ll just have to answer this question here, though I didn't get the answer, or several answers, till we arrived in the 'diggings.' There are several versions, but I'll give you the one that seemed the most authentic.

Swiftwater was in love with a young lady at Dawson who failed to get excited about him, and they quarreled. The next day she was seated at a table in a restaurant waiting to give her order, and as Swiftwater came in, he heard her o r d e r ham and eggs. He walked straight through to the kitchen and asked the proprietor how many eggs he had in the house. The proprietor said, "About three-fourths of a crate."

"How much do you want for them? Every one!"

"Two hundred and seventy-five dollars."

He picked up the crate, walked outside, and smashed them all on the ground. All to keep his lady friend from having eggs for breakfast.

She went out on the last boat. When he learned that she had gone, he followed her overland.

Yes, the report is, he found her at San Francisco. She turned him down again. Her next younger sister married him after a dowry settlement. She later divorced him on the grounds of an affair with a still younger sister.

This is just a report. If it does any of these parties an injustice, we are sorry. But we know you are curious about this. We were.

XI

FIVE FINGER RAPIDS

We had left Swiftwater and companion ten miles when we came in sight of Five Finger Rapids—a spectacular freak. A string of rocks crossing the stream like so many large box cars on a siding. At first sight from up stream, it looked like the whole river was blocked; but we knew that wasn't so. Swiftwater had told us to keep to the right side and pass through between the right hand rocks which were the largest and had the best and widest pass. He said we would find a drop of two or three feet in the water, but if we hit it fairly we would have no trouble. This drop was a miniature falls, where the water ran over some underlying barrier.

I think the water spurted through in five places along the barrier, and from this it got its name. But we had no time nor desire to prove this thought. As we shot through between those two rocks, the boat taking the dive successfully, with a plunge downwards and then up, it was like passing through a short narrow canyon. It was, probably, twenty to thirty feet wide, and the rocks towered up on both sides about the same distance, and were, perhaps, thirty feet long. Those rocks, clear across the river, were all about the same height, but not quite the same shape. The two, between which we passed, were somewhat rectangular, but those to the left seemed to be more triangular in form.

Getting through, we were off again with all haste. It turned very cold that night, and for the next three days the temperature reached to thirty and thirty-five degrees below zero.

Right along here, one of those cold mornings, we had not been running long, when, ahead on the right bank, we saw some Indians breaking camp. They were all in the canoe but one buck about thirty years old, and he was handing in the last packages. As he ran up and down from the canoe to the camp, he was singing in time with his steps, "Tal-a-lu-la, tal-a-lu-la, tal-a-lu-la, ty-uck-ad-u, ty-uck-a-du." We didn't know what he was saying, and don't know yet, but the blamed thing has run through my mind for thirty-eight years. I now pass it on to you, but don't get the lilt.

They were loaded and pushed off just as we arrived, and we drifted along-side for some distance. I had time, as we passed their camp, to learn something about making camp in cold weather. They had felled eight small spruce trees, laid the butts crossed on top of each other in the shape of an acute angle, four on either side, tops on tops, then banked branches about the butts, making a wind break on three sides. Then they had built a fire in front, between the tops.

As we drifted near them, making signs, and speaking a few words they understood of English, I noticed an old man and woman, the young buck mentioned, and a young squaw, perhaps his wife, a girl of perhaps eighteen, and several children.

The girl was quite comely, and what do you suppose she did? Pulled out a p i e c e of white lace, a spool of thread, a crochet hook, pulled off her mitts and went to crocheting—in thirty to thirty-five degrees below zero! Why? Perhaps to show white man her accomplishments. She had been outside to school, perhaps, and would make white man good squaw. The report was current that any Indian maiden could be had by presenting her father fifty to one hundred and fifty dollars, and she would be glad to live in "white man's cabin," because of the hard winter and shortage of food in the native villages.

I might tell you here how we m a d e camps in the snow and ice from the Rapids to Dawson. We had developed a system. The floating ice was getting more plentiful and troublesome. Camp had to be made with dispatch. I had developed into the cook, Harry ,the camp maker. Duncan took care of the boat and cargo. Every night the boat was unloaded and the outfit stacked up

71

safely on the bank. No agreement had been made about this arrangement. It just evolved.

I had two sacks, one full of food stuffs in small quantities, the other full of pans. As Duncan jumped on shore with the rope, making it fast to a tree on the bank, I jumped on shore with my two sacks under one arm, and the camp stove and two gold pans under the other. Harry followed with the tent and an ax. I climbed the bank and found a suitable place to hang the tent between two trees. We always tried to make camp where there were trees but were not always successful.

On the spot where the stove was to stand, I kicked the snow aside, threw one gold pan face down on the ground, set the other face up on top of the first, and set the stove on top of it. This arrangement kept the hot bottom of the stove from firing the dead needles and moss and smoking us out.

Harry threw the opened tent over me, and I pushed the three telescoped joints of pipe up through the pipe hole in the tent. This gave Harry and Duncan, who took a few minutes to help at this time, the cue on hanging the tent. They each took an end of the ridge rope and fastened it to the trees at the proper height.

I sat down in the snow in front of the stove, a foot extended along each side of the stove, opened the door, took out some of the wood and touched a match to the shavings. We always filled the stove ready for starting the fire before we broke the previous camp. I pulled out my pans and materials, and before Harry had the tent fastened along the sides, the smell of bacon was tempting his nostrils.

Duncan was unloading the boat, and as the shore ice froze farther out each day, he had more to cut away to let the boat sidle back away from the floating ice; but even then the ice would scrape the boat all night long. By the time Duncan had the boat unloaded, Harry had felled a tree, and they both came in with arms full of the pine-scented boughs, which they spread over the snow six to eight inches thick. They then brought in our bed rolls and used them for seats.

As the tent warmed up, I had to get on my feet, of course, for the snow about the stove melted. Supper was now ready in a good camp. You would be surprised how proficient we became. Running till the last minute, and stiff from our long cold rides, speed and proficiency became our second names. Inside of half an hour, we would be eating.

But this picture was not all rosy. We had run out of baking-powder back along the trail, and our flapjacks were pretty flat as a result. We did not take time to cook anything but flapjacks and coffee, and by the time we reached Dawson we were nearer starved than we had suspected. Only breakfast and supper now, no time to stop for dinner; if we got hungry we ate a frozen, unleavened flapjack and liked it, or tried to.

This recalls a very amusing incident. The third day of this cold spell, we were running along toward noon, and I had been pondering the 'no dinner and frozen flapjacks,' when I got one of those wonderful ideas. I said to the boys that if they would keep the boat straight, I would furnish them a warm dinner. They hooted at my crazy idea. I proposed placing the gold pans on the sacks of goods, as I did on the ground in making camp; placing the stove on top and wiring it to the sides of the boat; sticking up the pipe, and starting a fire in the stove. I would put the frozen, left-over bacon and flapjacks in the oven and warm them up. I would make coffee too, if they liked. After a good deal of argument, I got their consent. I fixed things all up fine, had the stove full of fire and smoke coming out the pipe like a steamboat, had the grub in the oven, and was putting it over on the boys with glee. They were pulling away and grinning at my success—I supposed. Maybe they had a hunch of a different nature, I don't know; but one of the most unlooked for things happened.

We were bowling along in great shape, when down ahead there appeared a long island covered with trees. We had passed islands before and had no alarm about this one. It lay in the stream where it made a quick bend to the left. As the ice flow reached these islands, it split, and at the bends, it usually ran the most heavily toward the bend side of the stream To avoid getting in the jamb, we usually took the opposite side of the stream and found clear water till the next bend, where we would cross over and take to the clear water again.

As we approached this island, it was difficult to decide which side of it to take, as the ice divided quite evenly. The boys kept the boat headed for the point of the island, and at the last moment, we all sang out, "To the left!" They pulled furiously to the left. It was a close call, and we were just getting our breath, when we ran right on to a shoot of water cutting through the end of the island. It was sucking in there like a mill race. We called these shoots "cutoffs." It was by the skin of our teeth that we got by without being drawn in and rushed down the shoot. We were complimenting ourselves on our narrow escape when we ran slapdab into another. There was no escape this time. Into it we went. The boys turned the boat's nose down it as the last precaution. But, happy days! Trees with their roots still in the banks were leaning over the surface of the rushing water. The boat shot under the first, but my stove pipe struck, knocked over the stove, the stove door opened and burning coals flew all over the boat. We all jumped to throw them out before they set us afire. The next tree slashed us good with its branches, and before we could straighten up, the boat plumped into the side of a sand bar or little island at the foot of the shoot. There we stuck, while the cakes of ice pounded the stern. The boys tried frantically to swing the boat off with the oars but could not do it. Finally, Duncan leaped over the prow, lifted it up and swung it off then jumped in.

74

We were floating with the ice toward the other shore, when Duncan said, "Let us land."

We worked our way through the ice to the shore, he jumped out and made the boat fast to a tree upon the bank. Then he got an ax and began cutting away the shore ice to let the boat sidle in.

"What are you trying to do?" I asked.

"I'm not going another damn step till this river freezes over!" he said.

About one o'clock, and every reason to make haste! We could not move him. Camp he would. We went to work to make a good camp. Lots of trees for fuel and bedding, it was a good place to camp. By two o'clock, as the sun came through the frosty air, it gave the finished camp a comfortable appearance.

Brother was not unreasonable as a rule. He, in fact, was much more reasonable than I. His judgement was always so quick and sound that he had been, all my life, my greatest man-admiration.

We had dinner, and afterwards, as we sat smoking, I mused out loud, "Two hundred miles from Dawson and camped till the river freezes over!"

Then to him, "We shall have a time, trying to get to Dawson with sleds cut out of the trees and with no metal shods, six hundred pounds to each load. Besides, this river always jambs back from below with the floating ice before it freezes. It will be some problem getting to Dawson under the conditions."

He said nothing, just sat and thought. Later, he said, "Let's take a walk down stream." We all went down the river bank about half a mile.

As we wandered down and back there were three boats, one a large scow, went flying past among the ice. As each passed, I would say, "That boat will likely get through before the river jambs, and we shall be here waiting till next spring."

On the scow, tied to the front railing, was a burro, looking ahead. He reminded me of "Washington Crossing the Delaware." He had a very brave appearance.

As we returned to camp, Duncan said, "Well, if the ice is still running in the morning, and you fellows want to go, all right, we'll go."

I could understand his reason for stalling. Should a boat get caught suddenly in the jambing ice, as the river jambed back, it would be just too bad. In fact, the whole outfit. men and all, would be lost. I never felt the seriousness of our situation, anywhere along the trail, as he did, but he was dead right.

XII

CAUGHT IN THE FLOE

The next morning we were ready to pull out at daylight. The ice was still moving. It was cold, and the trees were snapping. A heavy fog hung above the river, Along about ten o'clock we saw a boat tied up to the left bank where the water was free from ice. Up in some trees on the bank, there was a great smoke rising, and, being nearly frozen, we tied up and went over to the fire. We found a number of men toasting themselves before a huge fire they had started in a pile of drift-wood. They gave us a hearty greeting and an invitation to warm up. Directly, we observed a big pail on some coals, also a frying pan, both covered, and a large coffee pot. They looked mighty good, but they were none of ours. They set them off after awhile as we were talking. Then they removed the lids and we beheld the pail full of steaming beans and the pan full of biscuits. T h e y handed us each a granite pan and a spoon, with a "Help yourselves, boys." We did. Hot beans! Hot biscuits! Hot coffee! That was the best meal of my life. We never saw those men again to know them, but I hope they got rich in the Klondike and are still living and happy.

Thanking them and wishing them luck, we left, taking up our fight with the ice and current. It moderated that evening, and the weather was clear and not too cold the rest of the journey.

But a big fight was ahead. The river turned left and right, left and right, like a wriggling snake. It nearly made us giddy, as day after day, with short wriggling bends, we hurried down that swift running stream.

Every time we faced the left bank, the cold, snow-covered mountains rose up from the water's edge; and toward evening, they became very gloomy. As I sat in the stern looking at them, it seemed as though I were having a bad dream. I had never felt so lost and lone-

77

some. At every bend, we had to work our way through the ice to the opposite shore to gain clear water and keep up as much speed as possible. Otherwise, we would have been obliged to drift with the ice.

We had wondered where the ice came from. It didn't freeze on the surface because the only surface ice was that along the shore, and that stayed right there. As we considered this strange thing, we saw, every now and then, cakes of all sizes come up to the surface edge first and flatten out on the water. Some were coated with sand and gravel. In our careless deductions, we assumed it was the snow accumulations that formed the cakes. They were all quite soft when we first saw them come up but froze hard after floating awhile on the surface. That they were coated with sand and gravel did not occur to us as offering any light on the mystery.

We passed over many shallow riffles where the river widened out; the most conspicuous was Rink Rapids. As we ran over one of these one day, I happened to look over the side of the boat and got the surprise of my life!

I exclaimed, "Boys, this river is freezing on the bottom!"

"You're crazy!"

"Look overboard!" I shouted. They looked, but by that time we had passed the riffle and nothing could be seen. They gave me the laugh. "All right," said I, "you wait, and I'll show you!" We approached another riffle, and I was on the alert. Sure enough, we were plowing through a soft mass of snow-like substance which rose from, and was fastened to, the river bottom. I yelled, "Look over board!"

They looked, and continued to look till the riffle was past. Then, "Well, I'll be damned!"

The river bottom, as well as all the land in that country, is perpetually frozen, no one knows how deep. In summer, the top thaws out a foot or so, but the frozen bottom is always there, ready to freeze upward when the temperature again gets low.

CAUGHT IN THE FLOE

We were now better able to understand the phenomenon of cakes of soft ice coming to the surface in deep water, some covered with gravel and sand. They had become
bouyant enough, eventually, to break loose from the bottom and rise to the surface. Some turned bottom up,
showing the gravel; others did not. And this remarkable
performance is the reason the Yukon river jambs with
ice before it freezes over.

About fifty miles from Dawson, the river became so
full of ice we had to drift with the flow, pushing the cakes
from the boat with the oars to prevent its being crushed.
It was mighty fortunate for us the river did not jamb up
at this time. If it had, I would not be writing this today.
When we reached Dawson, our oars were nothing but
pointed sticks. The feathers, and part of the shanks, were
all worn away from pushing the ice back off the boat.

We drifted in the floe, I don't remember how many
days, but were finally approaching Dawson. We passed a
large, wooded island above the mouth of the Klondike
river. As we passed down the left side of the island, near
its lower point, we saw a number of men cutting logs on
shore. We also saw, below a rock point on the right shore,
rising straight up out of the water and stretching out
across the river from the base of this rock, what appeared
to be a dam; the water dropped over some submerged
barrier.

The boys on the island called to us, warning us to
work our way over close to the right shore. "If you don't
get in close to shore, you will never get into Dawson. The
river turns sharply to the left down there and then sharply back to the right. If you are not close to shore, the
ice will carry you off to the far side of the river! You see
that opening in the ice near the base of that rocky point
where the ice seems to separate? You hit that in the
middle! It is a drop of about three feet, but you'll make
it all right."

We thanked them and worked over, as they had
said. They called after us, "See that wide shore with

tents on, straight ahead? You better land there; it is better landing there than farther down. The camp there is Louse Town, or Klondike City, and it is this side of the Klondike mouth."

"Thanks," we replied.

We reached the open space in the falls and pitched over, down and up, safely, and directly we were standing on the wide shore they had mentioned. Men out for a boat ride of pleasure would hardly seek that three foot drop-off, amidst a jamb of ice floes, but we were, by this time, hardened river and ice men; it was all in the day's work.

And this is the Klondike!

Can you imagine our relief, this first day of November, 1897, at one-thirty? It was some relief, believe me! Nearly two months of continuous struggle, hardship and danger, on the seven hundred and fifty mile trail from Dyea to Dawson!

Were we thinking most of gold now? No! Gold did not enter our thoughts. We were simply enjoying that glorious feeling of relief!

XIII

DAWSON

This wide shore we were on was a wide stretch of gravel, now covered with snow, over which the river rose in high water. A number of new-comers had their tents pitched on this shore, and we set up ours beside them. This was a temporary arrangement.

Klondike City, or Louse Town, was only a few cabins back in the trees near the mouth of the Klondike river where it emptied into the Yukon. Across the Klondike river, and a half mile below, was Dawson. The Klondike was frozen over, and traffic was going back and forth on the ice.

We unloaded the boat and had some dinner, then Duncan and Harry took a stroll down to Dawson. Dawson was a settlement of several hundred cabins, the police barracks, some warehouses now nearly empty of provisions, an idle sawmill, some bunkhouses—hotels with no meals—and several saloons and dance-halls. There were no restaurants open as provisions were gone.

The main street was along the river bank, between the river and the business houses facing the river. I don't remember that they called the traffic lane Main Street, but there the main traffic moved back and forth.

Toward evening, Duncan came back with a barrel on his back, and when he set it down, I discovered it was three-fourths full of sugar cubes—a welcome find, indeed. He said, "I ran into Alex McDonald (King Alex) down there, and I gave him Swiftwater's note. He asked me what he could do for us, and I told him we would like to get next to some good placer ground where we could get a start."

Alex had said, "That's pretty hard to do. All known good ground is being worked. Would you consider working for wages at $1.50 per hour?

"No, we would like to prospect and take our chances."

81

"Well, I have claims 40 and 41 on Eldorado just above the falls, if you would like to try that, but no holes have been sunk above the falls yet, and it is not considered very valuable. Below the falls, of course, is the richest ground we have."

"Well, we will take a look at 40 and 41."

"All right, if you decide to try it, stake off a fifty foot strip, a lay, across either of those claims and go to work at fifty percent."

Then, turning abruptly, Alex had asked, "Can I do anything for you immediately?"

Duncan said, "Well, we could use some more grub, as we have only a light two-man outfit for three of us." Alex turned to a wall where dressed beef was hanging, saying, "Can you use some fresh meat?"

"Yes, indeed."

"Take a quarter of that." He shook a barrel standing on the floor.

"Can you use some sugar?"

"Yes."

"Take that." Then, "Some dried fruit?"

"Yes."

"Take a box of that." Then to a clerk, "What else have you?"

"Only flour," said the clerk.

"Take a sack of flour."

Duncan thanked him, and told him we would go and see 40 and 41. He then got the nearly full barrel of sugar on his back and came to camp. After supper he and Harry borrowed a sled and hauled up the rest of the stuff.

Duncan and I decided to go up to see 40 and 41 the next day, and incidentally, call on Winters, on claim 13, Eldorado, the same stream on which were 40 and 41.

The next morning we all went up along an island lying in the Klondike near the mouth and picked out a camp place on the upper end of the island in the trees. Harry would transfer our camp there while we two made the trip up the creeks.

We went up the Klondike about a mile and a half to the portage over to the Bonanza C r e e k, and up that stream to 13, Eldorado. There was a fine smooth trail up those streams, on the ice where the snow had been worn down by much traffic, but when we reached 13, we had walked twenty-two miles and were all in. We had Swiftwater's cabin pointed out to us and went over there. There was a man in the cabin cooking supper. We asked him if he was Winters.

He said, "No, but he will be here shortly, make yourselves at home." We threw off our packs and were glad to rest.

Winters came in after a while, and two other men also. We told him we had met Swiftwater and had a message from him and delivered the note. He was very glad to hear from Swiftwater and asked many questions. He received us very graciously and requested us to camp with him as long as we wished.

We had a most wonderful supper and learned how nearly starved we were after about twenty days on unleavened flapjacks and bacon. They had such a variety of food it was surprising, and I was ashamed to eat all I desired.

We talked unceasingly during supper and afterwards. There were so many things they and we wanted to know.

Winters was a fine-looking young man of twenty-three years, very pleasant, and a plunger, like Swiftwater. He had charge of fourteen men for Swiftwater, down below a couple of claims, for which he was paid twenty-five dollars a day. He employed, for himself, a cook at twenty-five dollars per day, and two men, working a hole in front of the cabin, at fifteen dollars per day each. These four men all lived in Swiftwater's cabin together.

Winters' story: "Last winter, I lived in Circle City three hundred miles below Dawson. I had nothing but beans, beans, beans, and nothing but beans, till I couldn't look them in the face. I came up here with my blankets and stopped a few minutes here on 13, watching the men work. Swiftwater was sluicing, and, after a while, he said, "Young fellow, do you want a job?" I said, 'Yes.'

"When can you start?"

" 'Right now.'

" 'Well, grab a shovel.'

"I grabbed a shovel and went to work, and at noon he told me to come up and have some dinner. At quitting time, he told me to come up to supper. I went right along working for him for one hundred days, boarding and living with him, too.

"One night, he said, 'Winters, how much do I owe you?'

"I said, 'I don't know, I have been working one hundred days.'

" 'Then I owe you fifteen hundred dollars, and I'll tell you what I'll do. There is a piece of ground on the down side of the cabin, forty or fifty feet square, it's not very good, and we were panning fifty cents a pan when we quit drifting that way. I'll sell it to you for your fifteen hundred dollars.'

"I said I would take it. I sank a hole in the middle of it and got ninety dollars the first pan on bed-rock. I took five thousand dollars out of that ground.

When Swiftwater was going out, he said to me,' I'll sell you this thirty feet square in front of the cabin for your five thousand dollars, and pay you twenty-five dollars a day to look after my men till I come back in the spring.' I took it and here I am."

Next morning, he took us down the hole his men were working in front of the cabin. It was twenty-nine feet to bed-rock. We went down a ladder on the side of the hole. He had a man on top working the windlass, and a man below loading the box, which was eighteen inches square on its top and ten or twelve inches square on the bottom, and a foot deep, approximately.

This was our first face-to-face meeting with the real thing, and we were all eyes. The gravel and sand, in sinking and drifting, had to be thawed out with wood fires, as all the ground was frozen, no one knew how deep. Drifting on bed-rock necessarily thawed four to six feet above bed-rock, and all of this had to be hoisted for a distance from the bottom of the hole.

Winters took a candle and went in against the working face and passed the light along the face of the frozen wall.

He said, "See, the pay streak is the first foot and a half above bed-rock in this piece of ground. The rest of the four to six feet of gravel thaws down, too, and has to be hoisted for a time. Can you see the pay?" He ran the light along the foot and a half next to the bed-rock. Could we see the pay! Nuggets were glittering all along the first foot and a half above bed-rock!

He took his pocket knife and dug into his hand seven nuggets, the largest as big as a big bean, and the smallest about the size of a pea. He put them into an empty tomato can, then asked his man if he had any loose dirt (gravel). He said he had a few shovelfuls. Then, going to the bottom of the shaft or hole, where there was a pool of water from last night's thawing, he washed out the gold and black sand with it, and dumped them into his tomato can. He washed seven pans in a few minutes.

Then we went up to the cabin. He put the contents of the can into a blow-pan, a piece of tin with its sides and one end turned up about an inch, the other, or narrow end left open or flat with the bottom. This he put on the stove to dry out.

After the stuff got dry, he picked the pan up, and, as he tapped on its side with his fingers, he blew on the contents, and the black sand, or iron sand, went out the open end and the gold remained. Some particles of gold went out with the sand, but not many. At the same time, from many blowings and being carried in on shoes, the floor glittered with particles of gold, but they paid no attention to that. He put the gold on the scales, and he had two hundred and sixty-seven dollars. We asked him how much he expected to clean up out of that piece of ground, and he said, "Eighty-five thousand dollars."

"What is your ambition when you get cleaned up?" we asked.

"Well," he said, "I drove a milk wagon in Seattle before coming up here, and I am going back to Seattle to buy me the finest team of horses and the biggest wagon I can get, and I'm going out to look for those blankety-blank-blanks of rich road-hogs that used to run me into the ditch, and I'm going to tear their wheels off!"

He had asked us the night before what he could do for us, and we had told him just what we had told Mc-Donald, that we would like to get a good piece of ground to work, or locate a good claim. He told us about the same thing McDonald had, that it was a hard proposition to find a piece of known good ground that wasn't being worked, and that the whole country was staked for two hundred miles from Dawson. That was very discouraging. Could he do anything else for us?

"Well, we could still stand a little more grub to give us a full supply for three men for the winter."

He said, "All right, I'll fix you up when you go back, and if you run short before you strike it, come again."

We went on up to 40 and 41, about seven miles, and looked them over. Duncan was convinced that any gold of consequence that had ever been in those two claims had been washed over the falls: and 39 below the falls was reported the richest claim in the whole Klondike, as evidence. The claims were quite flat but sloped gently toward the falls. We decided not to work them.

I visited those claims again toward spring, as I happened to be near there, and I found cabins and mines on them. I visited quite awhile with the men who had risked their all on them, and they told me that they had lost out. They had found only eight and ten cents per pan on bed-rock. We had lost nothing there.

Well, we went back to Winters and told him that we found it impossible to return to Dawson that day, as my

legs, after sitting about twenty days in the boat, were so
soft, that the trip up the twenty-two miles the day before
and fourteen that day had played them out. I could not
walk any farther.

He said, "Make yourselves at home." We did, and
stayed another night with him and spent a very pleasant
evening. The next day he sent a man to Dawson with us,
and he found us some more grub.

Harry had the camp all set on the island and everything moved over when we got back. As we sat around
the stove that night, we considered the situation and felt
that our reception by McDonald and Winters had been
of the best; and it seemed unthinkable that we couldn't
break into the game. But there we were: no good ground
in sight, as stated by two of the best authorities, and all
creeks staked for two hundred miles from Dawson.

The snow was piling up, and one was helpless off the
beaten trail. Besides, the only really rich ground reported
was mainly on Eldorado and Bonanza creeks. Some fair
reports from Hunker and Dominion creeks, but they were
one hundred to one hundred and thirty miles away. What
should we do? Duncan said he would scout up the creeks
again in the morning which he did. He did not get back
for two days.

He found some friendly fellows on 9 below Discovery
on Bonanza, and stayed with them two nights. They advised him to move up into a partly finished cabin on
Adams creek, and from there we could scout around and
be comfortably housed for such time as we found it de-
sirable.

They said that they thought they were doing well.
They had a 'lay' on No. 9 below Discovery on Bonanza,
and no doubt we would eventually find a good 'lay' near
by. It seemed the best we could do. We moved up there,
finished the cabin and made our permanent camp, for
that it proved to be.

XIV

WINTER QUARTERS

While we were moving up, the boys suggested that I stay at camp on the island and have the meals ready for them when they got back. It was seventeen and a half miles one way; and they would be tuckered out when they got back, even if they made only one way per day.

We had secured one sled six feet long, with steel shods, a Yukon sled; but we wanted two, and they suggested I go out and borrow another. I went out that first day but failed to get a sled; they were all in use. But in the evening I found a cabin back in the woods with a sled leaning up against the wall outside.

I went in and found an old man lying on a bunk. I told him we were moving up Bonanza and would like to borrow his sled a few days.

"Well, you can't have it! I don't lend my sled!" This in a very surly, quarrelsome voice.

All men in there were not friendly any more than they were outside. We had an opportunity to turn the tables on this old gentleman later on and did.

While I cared for camp and cooked, the temperature got down to thirty-eight degrees below zero each day, and forty below each night. The boys made a trip up and back in two days, and I was alone every other night.

Before crawling into my sleeping bag, I would fill the stove with shavings and wood, ready to start the fire by reaching out and lighting it before I got out of my bag in the morning. After I got the stove ready, I pulled my coat on, buttoned it up, pulled on my cap and went down into my bag, boots and all. Then I reached out and pulled the other boys' bedding over and banked it on top and around my bag. In this way I slept warm enough, but I couldn't move or turn over because of the weight.

In the morning, or when I couldn't stand the weight any longer, I would reach out and start the fire. When the stove got red hot, I would remove the outside weight and crawl out.

The boys found shelter in the cabin of our new friends on No. 9 the nights they stayed up there so we got by all right. The nights they were home we kept the fire going all night, one or the other reaching out and poking some wood into the stove when the fire got low.

While we were here on the island, brother Duncan had two night-mares. I was awakened one night by the most unusual noise in his sleeping bag. Scratching, clawing, and puffing like a b e a r had got in beside him. I reached out and unhooked the head flap of my bag to wake him up, then, when he awoke sufficiently to unhook his top and throw it back, he drew himself to a sitting position, puffing, blowing, and sweating.

"What's the trouble?" I inquired.

"My God, we were crushed in the ice."

He repeated this performance one other night.

The Friday morning after we returned from our first trip up to Nos. 13, 40, and 41, Eldorado, some men passing said, "Have you been down to see the river? It jambed this morning about two o'clock, and it's quite a sight. Those tents on Louse Town shore were washed away, and the boys had to wake up and hustle to save themselves."

Harry had finished moving Thursday, and Friday morning at two o'clock the jamb had taken place. Had our camp remained another night down there, we would have lost all. The water rose six to eight feet and covered that broad shore with ice.

I went down to have a look at the mouth of the Klondike. What a sight! The Yukon up and full of ice. Cakes standing mostly on edge, it seemed. And the ice was full of boats. Some standing on end, prows down, some the other way about, some on their sides, all fast in the jamb.

Out about fifty yards from shore with about a third of its prow end sticking up in the air, and several hundred yards below where we left it, there was a boat I suspected was ours. When the jamb froze so we could get out there, it proved to be ours.

It was rather a pitiful sight after the good service of these boats. Battle scarred as they were, we could have wished them a more pleasant place to rest. We had wondered sometimes how our boat had stood some of the crushing it had received from the ice. We discovered, when we cleaned it out at Louse Town, it had about four inches of ice in the bottom. It had leaked, or shipped, that much water, and it had frozen solid, which may have given it the needed strength.

I don't think I told you that the river had jambed two weeks before we landed and then broken loose again. It had, and that breaking loose allowed us to get in safely.

One boat with seven men rounded the point above Dawson in the ice before the first jamb. They couldn't get closer than about forty yards to shore as they passed Dawson. The men on shore got a rope and tried to throw an end out to them but could not reach them, and as the attempt was being made, the boat collapsed like an egg shell and went down, men and all. No one knew who they were. This accident accounts for seven of those men who never returned.

I was exploring the Bonanza bottoms below the portage one day about a week after the jamb, and there in the thick brush and trees I saw a new tent: I thought it strange, a new tent, and hidden back in the jungle. I worked my way to it and called.

A man opened the flap and said, "Come on in." I went in and was surprised to see practically nothing inside but a stove. I asked why they were so bare.

"O, we got caught in the jamb on shore at Louse Town and lost everything but our lives." They didn't seem to be grieving about it. They had money or friends —they needed no help. But after landing their outfit, with so much struggle, at its destination, to have it swept away was tragedy indeed.

Well, let us get back to moving. Duncan and I were going up the trail with the last trip. We had one sled with the heaviest load. Harry was on ahead with another sled they had borrowed up at No. 9. We were crossing the portage from the Klondike to the Bonanza. Duncan had the sled rope over his shoulders, pulling, and I was pushing, when we met a man tripping along with an empty sled.

The man stepped out of the trail himself but failed to get his sled all out. Just a slight oversight on his part, but it was so common an oversight that it became almost unbearable to those with loads. Duncan lost his temper, hit the empty sled a mighty kick, and raised it over into the deep snow, while the man with the rope around his neck came near going over with the sled. Duncan cussed and would have fought right then, had the fellow said a word. We went right on.

If we had known who that man was, we would nearly have taken him in our arms. We had been looking for him ever since we left home but did not recognize him.

We were finally moved and fixed up comfortably. We whip-sawed boards for the cabin door and a table, cut a piece out of a log in the wall and made a window. Along the back wall of the cabin, and four feet from the floor, we placed two poles: one, two inches, and the other, three feet from the wall, fastening the ends onto the side walls. Between these two poles, we hung our sleeping bags. They just had room, the cabin being fourteen feet wide.

The bags had leather eyelets along the sides for the purpose of lacing them onto something of this kind. We had ropes for the purpose. They made rigid hammocks. Then we took the sheepskin bag from inside, cut it down the middle, and made a sheepskin cover. We cut the brown cotton inner sheet bag down the side and made a sheet cover.

Those sleeping bags got our goat. We were always too hot or too cold, and one couldn't throw off the cover if too warm, nor add to, if too cold. In the cabin we would have about the same temperature always, so we made covers of the inner bags, and lay on top of the outer canvas.

Now a word about the window and cabin. We took a fifty pound flour sack, washed it clean, and stretched it in the place from which we had cut a piece of log about two feet long. When it dried, we painted it with bacon grease. The cold temperature kept the greased cloth like a kind of glass, and quite a little light came through.

The cabins built there were very fine: straight logs, laid on top of the moss, pressed down—the natural covering of the ground is moss—shutting out the bottom air completely. Then a layer of moss between the logs made an air tight wall. The cabins were so air tight that a ventilation box, with no top or bottom, was placed in the ridge about in the center, and a board damper, we'll call it, was hung in the middle of the box. This damper had a string on each side that could be pulled to close, open, or partly open, as desired.

For a table, we bored a couple of two inch holes in the wall and drove two pieces of wood with rounded ends into the holes. The pieces of wood were the length desired for the table. On top of these we nailed boards and had a table that wouldn't upset.

Now we were established but were more uneasy than at almost any other time. We must rustle, but how and where?

We had come several thousand miles, faced much hardship and many dangers, spent considerable money we could ill afford to spend, lost a year's time, at least, left families behind depending on us and betting on us. It was the crucial moment, but where was the spot to strike. There was gold in "them thar hills," all over the hills, in fact, but there were only a few spots worth striking. And that country was a big place. The snow was getting deep, and the temperature had gone down to fifty degrees below zero to stay. The mercury did not thaw out for two months, which requires warmer than forty below. The sun had disappeared, not to be seen again for two months. Our days were four or five hours of twilight. And, according to the best authority, "All known good ground was being worked, and all creeks were staked for two hundred miles from Dawson." Yes, and much more ground that wasn't good was being worked, but all the workers were millionaires, in their minds.

But where should we strike the blow? If we missed, all our sacrifice went for naught!

Go out and sink a hole! Yes, risk our all on one spot, with odds a million to one against us. It wasn't easily decided, and we wanted assurance.

I have set this down at length, not only as a defense in our case, but in defense of nearly forty thousand other Klondikers who failed.

Duncan and Harry took a notion to go up Adams creek and see if it were staked far up. We were camped about three-fourths mile from where it flowed into the Bonanza. They started out early in the morning and got back late at night.

Adams creek, they found, was staked clear to its source, but they staked two claims on the last ditch. There was not a soul on the creek above our cabin, and it was a long way to the source, and all staked. That meant no one else could work the creek, though the owners did not consider it worth while. That was one way the new-comer was blocked out. In the States, one might jump any claim not being worked, but in the Klondike the claims were recorded in the Canadian Government Office at Dawson, and the recording fee of fifteen dollars held the claim one year, another fee held it another year, and so on.

The boys had a big day's tramp through the deep snow and were all played out. They didn't get much inspiration from the trip. It didn't look good to them, no one working the creek, and no signs it had ever been prospected. But in the morning their enthusiasm returned.

"Who knows, these claims we staked may be full of gold."

They bantered each other, "Let's go and record them."

"I'll go you."

"Well, it we don't work them this winter, we may want to next spring."

They struck out for Dawson, another thirty-five mile walk. They paid fifteen dollars to record each claim, or thirty dollars for both. I don't know where they got the money, but I think Harry had that much in his boot. The Canadian Customs Officer had taken all that Duncan and I had.

They got back in two days, and we were just where we were before. "No, we can't go up Adams to prospect for the winter. It would be an awful task to get up there this winter and build a cabin. It would be staking our all on too slim a chance." This was the discussion, and the final conclusion. We would get out and scout up and down the diggings where things were doing and see if we could find anything.

We spent several days at that without anything gained but more information.

Then we hit on a happy thought. "This claim we are on extends only to the 'Rim'—where the valley bottom turns sharply up the mountain—and we can take a bench claim right here back of the cabin."

We would prospect it before recording to see if it were worth anything. We sank a hole about twelve feet deep and were stopped by a large boulder, part of a rock slide, and had to give that up.

XV

JUDGE OSBORNE

We continued our scouting. One day the boys had been offered a job for one man on No. 22 Eldorado. After talking this over, we decided one of us should take it for safety, while the others scouted around. We could all have gone to work for wages at any time, but we wanted something better than that. Considering the price of supplies, fifteen dollars per day was about the equivalent of three dollars back home, less than three dollars. Right here let me give you a bill of goods bought at Dawson, November, 1897. I have it recorded in my note book. It was an actual purchase (paid for later on after we had worked for wages). You can figure the wage value for yourself.

250	lbs. flour	$325.00
125	lbs. sugar	61.25
100	lbs. beef	125.00
24	lbs. dried apples	27.50
46	lbs. salt pork	58.00
33	lbs. beans	41.25
578	lbs.	$638.00

This bill shows how far a day's wages would go paying for food at an average of $1.10 per pound. Three dollars would buy, back home, much more than $15.00 would buy in Dawson at that time, and we didn't get excited about fifteen dollars a day. We had left a better proposition at home. Of course, if a fellow worked all winter at that pay, then took the earnings home, he would have from two thousand to two thousand five hundred dollars —a little stake, but not enough for the risks we had run. I got acquainted with several men who did this. It was playing safe. But the braver men took their chances, win or lose.

Duncan took the job on 22 as a precaution, while Harry and I continued to look around. I was coming down Bonanza one day and stopped on No. 5 below Discovery to talk to a man by the name of Curtis. He and his partner had lay No. 9 on No. 5 and would sell half, "As we can't work it all ourselves this winter," he said.

After several days' sizing it up, we decided to take it in the name of all three of us. We were a little suspicious because they had a hole down with only a small dump and didn't seem to be keeping very busy.

But Curtis was a grand liar: "We are getting all kinds of gold in that hole. We landed on the pay streak, and it's rich." We learned early not to believe Curtis. His partner, Lung, was a different type and said little.

There were a number of men working the rest of the claim who seemed to keep busy. Thought they were getting rich, at any rate, though we didn't quiz them all. It was just possible Curtis and Lung had sunk in the wrong place, And besides, was this not the famous Bonanza creek? We would try it on their terms. We would be out only the sinking of a hole which would be about three weeks' time and labor.

The terms were one thousand dollars to be paid from our first sluicing in the spring. They were to get our dump if we quit. They couldn't lose, and we couldn't lose much.

The claim belonged to a Mr. Fox, Mr. Lamb, and Mr. G. R. Dodson.

However, we had to get consent of the owners before consummating the sub-lease, and it meant a trip to Dawson. Curtis and I went to Dawson. We were unable to find any of the partners but left word we wanted to see one of them as soon as possible. We learned one of them was coming up the creek in a day or two, and we went back and waited.

A day or two later, Curtis and I were having a hot argument in his cabin, just about to fight, for I had called him a liar, which he certainly was. A rap came on the door, Lung opened the door, and there stood Fox. I told Fox I had accused Curtis of lying, which might account for any noise he might have heard.

Fox said, "Gentlemen, keep me out of this. I believe you wanted to see me."

"Yes, may Curtis and Lung sub-lease me half of their lay?"

"Yes, surely, if you can agree among yourselves."

"We'll try."

It took us several days to get over our mad spell, but we finally did and went down to Judge Osborne— hope I have spelled his name right—and had him make out the sub-lease. He wrote it with ink made from nail filings and vinegar, and my copy today looks about as it did the seventeenth of November, 1897.

On No. 6, below, on Bonanza, there was a man past middle life and his son, about twenty. They were the Osbornes. They had a lay. They had built a cabin and were working with all their might. We saw them every day. The Judge had been a heavy man when he started on the trail, but he had worked all the fat off. He was Judge Osborne of Seattle and had served eight years on the Supreme Bench of the State of Washington. He, like many others, was sure he had it in "the dump."

The Judge and his son were likeable fellows. They worked hard all winter. The last report I had of him was to the effect that he washed up about seven hundred dollars. Take away fifty per cent for the owners of the claim and what have you? Almost nothing.

The Osbornes got their wood supply up the mountain behind our cabin. Came every day or two. Went up the mountain side, cut several trees, and sent them down the skidway, then came down and laid the butts on the sled and made them fast with a rope. Then they were all set to go home. Sometimes the Judge would come to our cabin after he had his load to get a drink of water. It was quite a job to get those poles down off the mountain.

KLONDIKE DIARY

Harry had known the Judge in Seattle, but the Judge, of course, had not known Harry. He came to our door one day for a drink of water, and, as he was standing there, he looked longingly at a shank bone hanging under the porch roof. We had carved all the meat off that particular bone but had more of the quarter hanging there beside it.

The Judge said, "My, wouldn't that bone make a fine pot of soup!"

Harry said, "Yes."

I overheard the conversation and said to Harry, "Let the Judge take the bone, Harry."

The Judge protested he couldn't think of robbing us, but we finally prevailed upon him to take it along. After thanking us profusely, he went over to his sled, got the rope back of his neck and under his arms and went on down the trail with the bone in his hand.

Harry took a fit of laughing, and said, "By gar, wait till I get back to Seattle and tell about sending da Judge down da trail wit dat bone. By gar, dat is de funniest dam thing, har, har, har!"

We went at the lay, sank a hole, and got thirty-five cents as the richest pan on bed-rock. We never went back there to work. That thirty-five cents would never pay out. We had selected the best possible spot according to the advice of the old-timers. We had chipped with picks down through the frozen muck, eight to ten feet, then thawed the gravel to bed-rock at twenty-two feet. We were done with that.

Harry got a chance to join another man in working a lay on No. 8 below, and left us, which was all right. I was alone at the cabin and once in awhile I would run up to No. 22, Eldorado, to see Duncan. Sundays he would nearly always come down.

I finally got a strip of ground at the lower end of No. 6 from Ogilvie and McDonald. I had become acquainted with two men on the lay above mine, and they were, so they said, taking out from forty to fifty dollars a pan—were very enthusiastic. They told me just where to sink and hit the pay streak, as it was heading for that spot. They had come there the previous July, built a cabin, and were very comfortable, and had a dump out as big as a barn.

Well, I started to sink. Chipping, chipping the frozen muck with a pick. This muck is black and has some sand in it and took a lot of pick sharpening. That was all right with me. I had sharpened many a mine pick and knew just how to do it. The muck chipped in scales, just like ice, only tougher because of the sand. The holes were sunk three by six feet. Duncan came down on Sunday and agreed to come to help me when I needed the windlass.

I sank that hole plumb and pretty, t w e l v e feet through the muck, and struck the gravel. I needed assistance and went up to get Duncan. He was sick and looking tough, had not worked for several days. He told me to get some one else to help me.

That wasn't hard to do for men were running around loose, just as we had been. I went back down home expecting to go out in the morning and pick up a man. In the morning, I got out late and was going down the trail about ten o'clock, and I met Duncan pulling a sled up the trail.

When we left home, he weighed two hundred and ten pounds, was nearly six feet tall, and big-boned. Here, coming up the trail was not Duncan, but our old father, bent, and thin, his full beard some gray. His bent legs, that used to be so straight, were flopping outward at the knees at each step. I stood and tried to look at him but couldn't see him for tears. We went on up to the cabin in silence.

XVI

WE MEET REYNOLDS

We rested a few days while Duncan recuperated. In the meantime, we made a fine windlass. Then we went down and finished the hole. When we got to bed-rock, we scraped the bed-rock for the richest pan possible and panned out one dollar and twenty-five cents. This looks good, perhaps, for two shovelfuls of dirt; but, "Don't let us get excited." We didn't. We got down to figuring.

At that rate, we could expect to hoist, counting all four to six feet of top that would thaw down, which had practically nothing in it, about twenty-five dollars per day. Half of that went to the claim owner, one fifth to the government, our share of the dam, flume and sluice boxes to be deducted from the remainder. We got what was left. Our share of twenty-five dollars per day looked small when we could earn thirty dollars per day at wages. We didn't go back any more.

Before we sank this hole, Mr. Ogilvie, who, with Alex. McDonald, owned the claim, came to the cabin to see if I would work on cutting the foundation for the dam, along with several other men. This dam was to supply water for Nos. 6 and 7 claims, or one thousand feet of flume. We got all the foundation cut out in fourteen days; then it was left for the dam builders.

For this fourteen days' work, I was paid two hundred and ten dollars, or fifteen dollars per day. Duncan came down from No. 22 with over six hundred dollars, so that we had enough to take us out to the States, if we decided to go.

We had obtained a bunch of books and put in a while reading. One would read out loud by the bacon dip for an hour, then the other would read.

While we were doing this one day, Ogilvie came to the cabin to see if we would let the dam engineer camp

100

with us in the cabin. We told him to send him along, we had lots of room.

In a few days he came, and who do you think he was? The old snappy fellow that refused me the loan of his sled, when we were moving up from Dawson. I do not think he recognized me. And I never introduced myself. He camped with us two weeks, and we tried to make him feel at home.

* * * * *

Ogilvie had a squaw; some old sour doughs did. He was perhaps fifty years old, and she was about the same age. She would, every so often, get tired of staying in his cabin and go off up or down the creek for a time. In other words, she would run away. Any cabin where she could find lodgings was her boarding house for the night, especially if the boys had some liquor.

She ran away while we were cutting the foundation for the dam. Their cabin was only about thirty yards from where we were working on the dam. Ogilvie went to find her and in a day or two brought her back.

She was in the cabin only a short time when she came down to the dam, filled her apron from the pile of gravel we had thawed out, then said to us, "Watch me break Ogilvie's windows."

She went close to the cabin and began throwing the stones at the windows. Directly he came out mad, caught her by the neck and ran her inside. The curtain went down.

* * * * *

You remember I had a lay from Ogilvie at the bottom of No. 6, on which we sank the last hole; and the two fellows next had told me where to sink. They said they were taking out from forty to fifty-dollars per pan on bed-rock. They had a big dump, as big as a barn, as I said before.

The day or two before we struck bed-rock, I was there alone. Just as I was about to go up for dinner, one fellow, about fifty years old, came up out of their hole with a sack over his shoulder, with about a pan of dirt in it.

He called to me, "The pay streak in our hole, that was running toward you fellows, has turned. I don't think you are going to strike it."

I thought, "You are another liar," but I tried to look disappointed. I went over to talk to him, and we both walked together out to the trail.

As we were separating to go to our different cabins, he said, "Come up to my cabin, and I'll show you how our dirt is panning out. I have a test pan in this sack."

I went along, thinking, "I'll be a sucker till I see what you are up to."

In the cabin, he very methodically dumped the dirt out into a pan, dipped it into a tub of water, gave it a few whirls, and nuggets were showing right now.

I said to myself, "Salted! What's his game?"

He washed out about fifty dollars, then, very unconcernedly, he said, "Yes, it has been running like that all winter; we've a fortune in that dump."

I said, "That's fine."

"But," he said, "we've got to sell out and will take only seven thousand dollars for the whole works, cabin and all. I have had word from my folks; they are having all kinds of trouble, and we have just got to go out."

I thought, "No mail has moved from nor to Dawson this winter, but you, of course, have had word," but I said out loud, "That's too bad you have to sacrifice like that."

"Yes, it is, but we have just got to do it. Will you take it?"

"How can I take it with no money?"

"We will take your note. Pay when you clean up."

"How can you get your money?"

"We'll cash the note at Dawson."

I didn't take the dump for seven thousand dollars. Did I lose a fortune? No, indeed!

But he must have tried that on others, for it got to Ogilvie's ears, and about three days after he had tried it on me, two Mounties dropped in on him from Dawson.

"We want to see your winters' test pannings," they said.

He took down a bottle from a shelf and said, "Here they are." The bottle had about fifty dollars in it. What he had washed out for me, I presume.

"But," they said, "you have been panning forty to fifty dollars all winter, where is it, the rest of it?"

"Why, it's in the dump, of course! This is only our last pan!" The police could do nothing and went away. If he had thrown it in the dump, that was fair enough. It would be there for the spring clean up.

Whom do you suppose they sold it to? Ogilvie and McDonald. For seven thousand dollars!

What did the dump clean up? Just seven hundred dollars! Can you beat it? Two old-timers getting skinned like that!

Early in February, we heard much chopping going on over in a ravine a short way from our cabin, and we couldn't figure it out. But the third day of this chopping, we had just had dinner and were lying in our hammocks, smoking, when a rap came on the door. We called, "Come in."

The door opened, and who do you suppose stuck his head in the door? The man whose sled Duncan had kicked off the portage trail.

He said, "May we come in and warm up our lunch on your stove, and eat in here."

We said, "Surely, come in."

"There are four of us."

We answered, "Come on in."

He came in and began to warm up their lunch, saying, "The other boys will be here in a minute."

It was remarkable how changed in appearance most Klondikers became, with long hair and beards, t h e i r faces weatherbeaten and their weights altered. Their own folks would not have known them, if they didn't speak.

Soon another man came in, a big heavy man and said, "The other boys went down to the cabin below." He picked up one of our chairs, a block sawed from a log, set it in the middle of the floor, and sat down. Then he pulled off his cap and threw it back against the wall, pulled out a stub of a pipe and filled it with tobacco, took a match from his pocket, and stepped over to the stove to strike the match. We watched him closely.

Then the usual question, from Duncan, "Where did you fellows come from, outside?"

The big fellow said, "I came from LaSalle, Illinois, and my partner came from Morris, Illinois." He had struck his match and was applying it to his pipe as he turned toward us.

"Isn't your name Reynolds?" we both shouted at once.

"Yes, but who the hell are you?" he shouted back.

"Our name is Medill," we said.

"Well, I'll be blankety blank!" he shouted, "I didn't know you were up here."

We belonged to the same lodge of Masons in LaSalle and knew each other well. Maybe we were not a happy bunch of sourdoughs!

Reynolds had left home two weeks before we had, and we had been on the lookout for him all along, had inquired for him a hundred times up and down the trails, and here he was.

Holderman, Reynold's cousin and partner, was a stranger to us. Whether he recognized Duncan as the man who had kicked his sled, we never knew. At any rate, it was never mentioned by either.

When the excitement died down, we asked, "What are you fellows doing?"

"We are getting out logs to build a cabin here on No. 7. We have taken a lay. We took up a bench claim down the Bonanza and sunk some holes but got only eight to ten cents a pan and gave that up."

"Have you prospected No. 7?" we asked.

"No, but two of our friends from Utica, Illinois, have a string of dumps on the next lay, and they assure us the pay is there all right. They have made it big. They say their dumps are full of gold. By the way, maybe you know them, the Taylor brothers."

"No, we are not acquainted with them." Utica is about four miles from LaSalle.

"Well, they may know what they are talking about," we said, "but we would suggest that you sink a hole before you build your cabin. We sank a hole on No. 6, and frankly, we are skeptical. Besides, this is an awful time to build a cabin."

"We must have a cabin. We have no place to stay."

"Stay with us till you prospect it. We have lots of room here."

"Oh, there is no doubt about striking it. The Taylors are terribly excited about what they have done, and our lay is next to theirs. We might accept your hospitality till we build the cabin, but we will strike it all right. The Taylors are not mistaken."

"Well, stay with us till you build."

They stayed with us for two weeks; then, as they had finished their cabin, they left. Two weeks later, we went down one Sunday to see how they were doing. They were quiet.

"How did you make out in your prospect hole?" we asked.

"No good, we've quit," they answered. "And we are afraid the Taylors are going to get a surprise."

The Taylors washed out in spring two thousand two hundred and fifty dollars. They had worked since August or September, paid their share of the dam and flume, and furnished their sluice boxes. They got half or one thousand one hundred and twenty-five dollars. They had used up their year's grub-stake, and had five hundred and sixty-two dollars and fifty cents each, minus their expenses and other necessities.

Our deduction was, that, outside of the very rich claims on Eldorado, thirty-nine in all, with a few scattering over other sections, the only men who made good were the claim owners. They got half of the output. Occasionally, on the rich claims, they got sixty per cent. The lay workers got the balance and paid all the expenses.

It was unbelievable, the confidence those poor fellows had in their dumps. One fellow on No. 7 below, I remember well, but not his name, expressed this confidence for all in his often repeated exclamation, "I'm a Skookum King!"

I have here before me a page from "The San Francisco Call" of Tuesday, April 19, 1898. The whole page is a summary of the output of the Klondike for the spring of 1898 cleanup, written up by Sam Wall, in which he states he visited each claim and got an accurate statement from the workers of each claim of what they would clean up. He states it was the only way to get an accurate estimate of the output for that spring.

His "accurate estimate" was all wrong. He got his "estimate" before the cleanup, when every worker was full of that confidence in his dump that I have mentioned. After the cleanup, if he had made the same "careful examination," he would have found the workers pretty much silent.

There was lots of gold taken from the Klondike; but those who produced it did so at a big loss, and the claim owners, who did little or none of the work, walked off with the big money.

* * * * *

The last Sunday I walked up the creek a ways with Duncan, as he was returning to No. 22 Eldorado, we were passing over about No. 2, Bonanza, when Duncan pointed over to the mountain on the right hand and said, "Do you see the depression up on that hill side? Well, when

I quit my job on No. 22, I'm coming down and we'll sink a hole right in the middle of that depression. Any gold sliding down the mountain was caught in that pot-hole." It looked likely, and I agreed.

The last time I went up to get him to come down and help me on the last hole we sank, what was my dismay to see a windlass going up on that depression. I went over and found two fellows had a hole down in the center of the depression. Their stakes took in all the depression, one hundred feet square, and the land all around their claim was staked by others. There were a number of men standing about watching the boxes being dumped, and every box showed gold a plenty.

I picked up a nugget, about a half-ounce, and after looking at it a while, I handed it to the windlass man and said, "Here's a nice one." He looked at it a moment then threw it on the dump among the gravel. They had been offered ten thousand dollars for the claim when they struck bed rock and had refused the offer.

Well, it wasn't ours. I suppose the lucky boys felt good and probably needed it, too.

XVII

SWEDE CREEK TRAGEDY

Most of the claim owners seemed to be quite satisfied with the honesty of their workers and made no check against what might be filched. It was a difficult matter to prevent the pannings, or a few nuggets, going into secret hiding places. And I have an idea some of it disappeared in that manner. There were some owners, however, who were disliked because of their parsimonious conduct.

Claim No. 7 was owned by an ex-barber, and he came around every month to collect the test pannings. His habit of taking in dimes had followed him into the Klondike; and the workers expressed their disgust to others, if not to him.

The pannings were usually collected and kept in the cabins for the final settlement, but any gold in the dumps was there to stay till cleanup. About half an hour after the warm gravel was dumped on the pile, it was frozen so hard it was safer than in a bank. It had to be thawed out again before the gold could be separated from the gravel, and that required spring sunshine.

When the sun came back in the spring, the sluice boxes, about a foot square, were run from the flume past the side of the dump into a larger box, from which led two or three lengths of foot square boxes whose bottoms were cleated to catch the gold as the water carried it through. Into this large box, or tub, the dumps were shoveled as the sun thawed them out. A man stands in this tub, with a big fork and throws out the gravel. The gold settling is caught by the cleats in the final boxes.

Bonanza creek valley, or canyon, was a queer sight toward spring. Looking up or down the canyon one beheld the whole bottom full of dumps. These dumps looked like nothing so much as huge straw stacks covered with snow.

And such a strange snow I had never seen. It got to
be about three feet, or more deep on the level. Over
mountain and valley alike. The mountains had no more
than the valleys. It was a kind of frost snow. A white
smoke snow. It was so light and dry that one's feet went
to the ground at every step. One just pushed through it
and walked on the ground. As he did so, it flew up in his
face like a cold fog. When we would chop down a tall
slim spruce with its short limbs, it all disappeared into
the snow but the tips of the uppermost branches. It gave
one a queer sensation. Then we trimmed the limbs off by
feeling for them with ax or foot to get their location.

We thawed ice for water. All small streams froze to
the bottom. We cut a trench across this creek of ice, then
dug a chunk off as we needed it, broke it into small
pieces, and thawed it on the stove. We had a tin dish
pan; I don't know how we came to have it, but we used
it to thaw ice, and it was one of the curios we showed
visitors. It rusted on the bottom, and each rust spot became a hole after a while. We had a quantity of carpet
tacks, and, as a hole appeared, we cut a tack close to the
head and riveted it in the hole. By spring, the most of
the bottom of the pan was tack heads.

Candles cost a dollar apiece and couldn't be had at
that, as a rule. We took a rifle shell, split its mouth in
three parts about an inch down the shell, bent these
pieces outward and they made three legs. We unraveled
a piece of canvas and got enough string to make a wick.
We placed this contraption in a baking powder box lid,
filled the lid with bacon grease, and had a very good
bacon-dip light.

A half-pound baking powder box we used as a lard,
or grease, can. Its most important use was to keep the
camp in amusement. One or the other of us would grab
the frying pan and begin the making of flap-jacks. We
always put in lots of grease; it helped flavor the jacks,
and in that cold country one relished lots of fat. The extra grease in the pan was always poured back into the

can. That is, we poured more in the pan than was necessary, then poured it back into the can, leaving what stuck to the pan as the required amount. By and by the can became very hot. The cook picked it up in a hurry. It burned his fingers and usually dropped to the floor, spattering its hot, disagreeable contents all around, to the cussing of the cook and the howls of mirth from the others. It seemed like we couldn't remember that can got hot. We couldn't throw it away; we had nothing else for the purpose.

Along about the middle of February we were getting short of some things in the food line. We were getting tired of mouldy corn meal cooked with dried apples and water. We thought one of us should make a trip to Dawson to see if any changes could be found. I agreed to make the trip.

I left camp on February 21. It was forty below zero, which was fine. I took some grub in a sack over my shoulder, as was customary when expecting to be out more than a day. I also took something to cover my face if it got colder.

Those who could afford it wore a parka with hood attached. This was a fur coat with fur hood. The hood, when in place, extended in front of the face in a kind of tube, and the warmth of the face kept the frost back. It was very fine equipment for that climate.

I got onto the Klondike river about dusk, had felt comfortable all the journey of fifteen or sixteen miles. But, as I came out on that stream, I felt a slight breeze coming up the valley. It didn't feel bad on my face, and I went on down the trail, but soon I passed two men, and I heard what I had heard often before. I had said the same thing to others occasionally.

They said, "Your face is frozen, sir."

"Thanks," I replied. The first and only time either Duncan or I had been frost-bitten.

I turned into the first cabin on the left and rapped on the door. They said, "Come in." I opened the door

110

and threw in my sack, then closed the door and rubbed my face with snow. They, thinking this a strange act, opened the door to see what was wrong and found me rubbing my frozen face.

"Yes, your face is frozen," they said, as I stepped into the cabin, "and it's cold. It's sixty-eight below zero." I covered my face and went on into Dawson. That night, after my face thawed out in the bunk-house, the water ran from the blisters. The next morning I was a sight.

I still had a full beard. We had thought a beard would protect our faces, but we should have taken our cue from most old-timers who were clean-shaved. My worst frost-bite was along my jaws, and for two weeks, I had to sleep on my back to keep my whiskers from touching anything. Scabs formed all over my face and in my whiskers, but, believe me, when my face got well, off came those whiskers.

The next day, February 22, it was seventy-two below zero! I foraged around from cabin to cabin, picking up one thing here, and another there, where there was a surplus. One party would send me to another who had something to spare. In this way I spent the two hundred dollars I had brought with me, but by the break in the scales I received only one hundred and eighty-five dollars worth of stuff. You see, every one had a scale for weighing gold and could manipulate his own scales so he would not lose, it being customary to give your sack to the man of the house; he weighed the gold.

The first time I saw money change hands in Dawson impressed me. I was in one of the big trading company's warehouses. King Alex was there and was talking to the clerk through the window in the wicker work over the counter. On a broad shelf along the wall behind stood a large delicate gold scale in full view. I guess it would weigh an eyelash.

Alex asked if there was any whiskey in the house.

The clerk said they had about half a barrel.

111

Alex said, "We're having a little party tonight and I guess that will do." He pulled a fifteen thousand dollar gold sack from his outside coat pocket. It was about one third full. Giving it a swing, he sent it through the open window, thudding against the wall beside the scales. The scale needle, about two feet long, vibrated violently.

The clerk smiled, took the sack, and poured gold in the pan till the needle pointed to the right spot, then tied the sack and passed it back to Alex.

There were a lot of men staying around Dawson watching the recorder's office; and, when anyone came in to record a claim, these stampeders got the location and were soon off for that creek to stake claims. They usually had a sled all hooked up with camp outfit ready to go. But this cold spell fooled a bunch of them badly. It was slightly mild just before the cold spell, and two Swedes came in to record claims on a little stream coming into the Yukon about fifteen miles above Dawson on the far side of the river. Being so close and so mild, they expected to make the stampede and return by night. They struck out without any provision to camp. They found water on the ice below the snow on Swede creek, supposedly from some kind of warm springs. The first thing they knew they got their feet wet, and, as a result, seven were brought in to Dawson frozen to death. They were bringing them in when I was there. I saw one of them pulled in on a sled under a blanket.

The two nights I was in Dawson I put up at a large two-story log bunk-house that stood facing the river. There were sixty-one bunks, single and double, most of them in the big room upstairs. They were made of boards with a handful of hay covered with a blanket for a mattress, and a blanket for a cover. But, as the fires were kept going night and day, one slept quite comfortably. They charged one dollar and fifty cents for a single and two dollars for double bunks, which was quite reasonable that winter when prices were so high. Of course, they got extra by the break in the scales balance. The house was always full.

I don't remember the name of the proprietor, but I can see him yet. He was an unusual type, hard to describe. About six feet tall and two hundred pounds weight. A wide face with yellowish skin, I would say, a half blonde. He had the wildest bush of dirty-colored, half-yellowish hair imaginable. It would never stay put. Then he was clean shaven. He looked like a wild crazy man to me, but he was not crazy by any manner of means.

He told his story to me and another fellow:

"I came over the Chilkoot trail last spring with six hundred dollars, two dogs, and a sled. Came on down here, hired a bunch of men to get out the logs, and built this bunk-house. Today, I am a wealthier man than any of my relations, who always called me a 'no-good.' I can show them today not less than forty thousand dollars and when I go out, if I ever do, oh boy, I'm going to make them sit up and take notice."

I started for home at seven o'clock, the twenty-third. It was seventy-two below zero, no wind, and a clear moon. I had gone about a mile up the Klondike when two young fellows passed me tripping along quite lively. They were wearing moccasins and parkas.

As they passed, I overheard one of them remark, "There is a fellow who will freeze to death."

I smiled under my face gear and frozen features. I knew why he had reached his hasty conclusion and was satisfied he had "reasoned with out his host." He saw my canvas coat and my leather shoes. But he didn't know about the wool shirts I wore below my sheep-skin lined, canvas coat, and my shoes that were two sizes too large and stuffed with woolen socks. He also didn't know that I knew I must not sweat. Sweating in that temperature was fatal. One would freeze right now if he got his underclothes damp and couldn't find shelter or build a fire. To keep from sweating, I had to move very slowly because of the amount of clothing I had on.

I was pulling a sled with something over one hundred pounds on, but I scarcely felt the pull, because of the slickness of the trail and shods.

By agreement, Duncan was to meet me at the nine-mile cabin at noon. He didn't find me there at noon and became alarmed. He met me about one and a half miles below the cabin. He said, "My God, I thought the cold had got you when you hadn't shown up at the cabin at noon."

"Oh, I took it easy," I said.

I had made seven and a half miles in five and a half hours on a smooth trail and hadn't dampened my underclothes a particle. I was very comfortable.

Duncan took the sled, though I protested there was nothing to it.

When we reached nine-mile, he asked me if I didn't want to go in and warm up.

"No," I said, "I would rather go on."

We went on. Within a mile of our cabin we met Harry, pulling a heavy sled. He was bound for another cabin and refused our invitation to camp with us for the night. He would rather go on while he was hooked up. He would make it, he said, but we never saw him again.

We reached home about eight o'clock that evening. We had been on our feet without resting or eating for thirteen hours. Of course we were some tired and hungry. I drank seven cups of coffee for supper!

After supper we examined the contents of my sled load. As I pulled out one thing after another, Duncan would express his delight. Finally, getting a can of tomatoes under one arm and a can of cabbage under the other, he went waltzing around the room to a tune of his own, singing, "I am a Skookum King!"

I will list some of the provisions I had gathered:

Bacon, forty pounds	$60.00
Two small cans Eagle Brand milk	4.00
Two lbs. McDonald plug tobacco	12.00
Two cans tomatoes	2.50

Two cans cabbage	2.50
Two cans plums, size of tomato cans	2.50
One two-pound can butter	4.00
One can dried vegetables	1.50
One fifty-pound sack flour	75.00

The tobacco was for Duncan particularly, as he had been a heavy user, while I had not. Of course, he insisted I help use it. That McDonald was plug but was used for smoking. One whittled it off with a knife and rubbed it between his palms to crumble it. Then he had fun trying to keep it lit. It was "old country" right. I guess we got our money's worth.

I want to speak of that can of butter. It weighed two pounds and was the best butter I ever ate. It had all the flavor of freshly churned butter of the highest grade. When we opened the can, it filled the cabin with aroma.

XVIII

ODDS AND ENDS

We spent the next couple of months in various ways, mostly watching the clean-up.

And while waiting these two months, this may be a good time to record some of the sights and incidents that belong to that far country and to this tale.

Our friend Reynolds wanted to sink a hole on the top of the mountain in front of our cabin. Holderman would not join him in what he called "That crazy stunt." But Reynolds was a very determined man, and he and Holderman fell out. I did not know many partnerships in that country that did not break up on the trail or inside. The conditions were trying; everybody got on the other fellow's nerves.

Reynolds hooked up with a man by the name of Kincaid, and they started to sink on the top of the peak. Reynolds came to our cabin nearly every day for a few minutes, and we tried to discourage him at the start, for it was a tremendous task climbing to the top of that hill each day and back down. Then, we pointed out, there was no water up there and all the stuff would have to be brought down to the creek.

No use to talk to Reynolds when he got set.

He and Kincaid climbed every day and discovered a very interesting fact. They sank through muck like that down in the valley, and struck gravel. They struck gravel, about ten feet of it, on the point of that hill. How did it get there? It had been carried there, or it wouldn't have been there. They found colors down through the gravel the same as in the valleys. They found bedrock where the deposit of gold was the thickest, same as down in the valley, but their best pan on bedrock was between eight and ten cents so they quit.

116

Now for the theories of how the gold got all over that country. To my knowledge there has never been a ledge found around there. The gold and gravel must have been carried to that country, but how. What seemed to be the best theory was this: Some time in the great past that country had been below the sea, as have been, probably, all parts of the earth, and while there, icebergs carried the stuff over what is now raised land and, being caught by the hill tops below, remained to thaw out and drop their loads.

* * * * *

An old, rotten, fallen down windlass on a prospect hole on one of the creeks was a monument to the efforts of some gold seekers years before. They had sunk to bedrock and finding nothing gave it up at that; but in the drifting of 1897 the miners found that the former prospectors had missed the pay streak by only two feet. The earlier workers may have passed away without ever hearing of the big strike of 1896. Almost every one can look back and see where some slight change would have altered his whole life for the better if he had only known.

* * * * *

I must not forget dogs. Of all things, dogs were the most wonderful part of that wonderful country, all kinds of dogs. But the native dogs were the most interesting.

We first ran onto dogs on the Chilkoot trail. Here we found them at work in earnest. They seemed to like work, and with what a solemn and dignified air they performed! They seemed to challenge the world to lay a finger on the goods intrusted to their care.

Up the trail comes an Indian family: a father with a huge pack on his bowed back, a mother with as large or larger pack, five or six children all carrying packs, then four to six dogs all carrying packs. It was surely a packing outfit. Saddle bags of interesting design hung over the dogs' backs; they were made of canvas, suitable in size to each dog. Holding the bags to each dog were bellybands underneath; forward straps to a collar, and breeching behind, simple but effective. The dog might fall into a hole of any kind, still the bag stuck to him. These bags were stuffed full of merchandise of various kinds and had flaps buttoned over the mouths of the bags.

Arriving at Dawson, we found dogs in teams of from one to fifteen, pulling sleds on the trails any and all times, day or night. There were no dogs running loose like we find in the States. Dogs were valuable; hence they were taken care of. Their usual value was placed at one hundred and fifty dollars each the winter of '97 and '98. We tried to buy two in February, advertised far and wide that we would pay three hundred dollars for a pair, but got no offers.

I was coming down Bonanza one day and ran onto what I thought were the most wonderful three dogs I had ever seen. I had seen them several times before, but they had been traveling and I could only stand and, with a thrill, watch them go by. This day I found them standing still; I walked up to them. Their owner was loading poles onto a bob-sled made of two six-foot sleds. He had stakes on the sides of the sleds and was laying the poles between them.

The three dogs stood there in all their wondrous beauty, lined up one before the other in the traces. They were by far the largest and most beautiful canines I had ever seen. I am sorry I didn't get more information about them as to breed, height and weight. Will just have to give you my own estimated description. They were about thirty inches high at the shoulders, heads a foot higher, thirty-six or more inches long, and weighed much more than one hundred pounds each. They had the most beautiful hair, three to four inches long, wavy and colored from a white to a deep tan, the color blended with no definite demarkation. They had very large, fine, intelligent heads, with ears short and cocked forward like collies. They were exactly alike and must have been from the same litter, but I do not know the breed.

DYEA—START OF DYEA TRAIL

Courtesy of Roger Dudley

DYEA TRAIL—STOPPED FOR A FALLEN HORSE

ACTRESSES FORDING DYEA RIVER

BUSY PLACE ON THE TRAIL

CANYON SOUTH FROM STONE HOUSE

CHILKOOT TRAIL—PASS IN THE DISTANCE

CAMPING AT THE FOOT OF THE PASS

PACKING ON THE TRAIL

AT THE SUMMIT

OVER THE SUMMIT—CRATER LAKE

CHILKOOT PASS WITH THE SNOW Courtesy of Roger Dudley

BOAT BUILDING AT LAKE BENNETT

WHIP SAWING

MILES CANYON

Courtesy of Roger Dudley

WHITE HORSE RAPIDS

Courtesy of Roger Dudley

FIVE FINGERS RAPIDS

Courtesy of Roger Dudley

ACTRESSES AT HAPPY CAMP

Courtesy of Roger Dudley

DOGTEAM AT DAWSON

ADAMS CREEK—OUR CABIN

BERRY'S CLAIM ON THE EL DORADO

WAITING FOR THE MAIL AT DAWSON—1898

ICE ON SHORE OF THE YUKON NEAR DAWSON

I asked their owner what price he had on them. He replied, "No price at all. They are not for sale. I have a standing offer of one thousand dollars any time I wish to take it, but am not taking it. Have had several offers of one thousand dollars."

I was going to Dawson one day, and, as I came out on the bank of the Klondike, there was a team of nine native dogs with sleds behind just coming off the river on to the one hundred foot grade leading up to the portage over to the Bonanza. The sleds were heavily laden, and, to give them an understanding of the seriousness of the pull ahead, the driver uncoiled his long whip, making it whine and snap along the sides of the team as he yelled, "Mush!" but never touching a flank. The team ran and struck the grade on the lope, but when the full weight of the sleds hit the grade it slowed them to a crawl.

As those dogs slowed down and found themselves almost defeated, they got down on their bellies, stuck all claws into the hard snow, and began to whine like their hearts would break. Grabbing tree roots that stuck out of the snow with their teeth, they pulled till their eyes stuck out; and those sleds **did not stop** till they were safely over the knuckle. I was breathless from sympathy.

There was a little fat lady, past middle age, I would say, who ran up the trail from Dawson once a month. She was said to have interests up some of the creeks. She drove one large Newfoundland dog to pull her sled, but the interesting feature of her outfit was the sled and how she rode it. She had a box with a high back built on the sled, had a box full of fine fur robes, and she was buried in the robes with only her parka-covered head sticking out. I met her on the trail several times, and always she would call "gee" to the dog, give me half the trail, while her rosy-cheeked face broke into the sweetest smile.

There was another lady who ran a dog team of two Newfoundlands. She hauled freight up and down the trail at so much per pound. She could be seen almost any day going or coming with her team and sled. I passed her on the trail many times.

I presume you know what a gee pole is; however, it is a pole about six feet long, bolted to the front of the right hand runner of the sled, and the fore end rising to the hand of the driver. By means of this pole, the driver, trudging behind the dogs, steers the sled. The dogs are hitched to the sled by a single rope reaching out beyond the driver and gee-pole.

One cold day of fifty-five below zero, while coming down Bonanza, I saw a team of fourteen dogs pulling two loaded sleds. Just before I approached, the driver turned them off to the side of the trail. Stopping them, he went up to a cabin. Immediately the thirteen native dogs curled up on the snow like balls of fur, but the fourteenth dog was a short-haired pointer bird dog from the outside. He was hitched about the middle of the team and had to stay. But that dog was cold! He just couldn't take it. With his back humped, his teeth clattering, and whining a chattering song like a lost monkey, he swung this way and that, back and forth. While I sympathised with the poor brute, I was ashamed that I laughed at him, but he was funny.

They told interesting stories about lead dogs. The quickest, most intelligent, best trained dog was put at the head of the team. He was a proud dog, seemed to understand he was in a position of importance. Often when some trouble arose among the other dogs, if they refused to pull, got into a fight or other difficulty, the lead dog would turn on them like a sergeant of infantry and straighten them out. But once a lead dog, he was spoiled for a rear position; he would sulk, he felt disgraced.

* * * * *

One of the richest men up there was Alex McDonald, called King Alex because of his wealth. He had interests in more than one hundred claims. I have mentioned him before. He was distinguished in appearance also, a little out of the usual. His six feet or more of height, two hundred pounds or more of weight and erect carriage would attract attention anywhere.

He wore suits of the finest wool with short jacket, no coat or parka, nor fur of any kind. He always wore a cap and moccasins.

He never carried anything, never drove a dog team, never pulled a sled. With his hands in his jacket pockets, he strode the trails with a light, springy stride. In this manner, he made the rounds of his interests every so often, about three hundred miles the round trip from Dawson. Having accommodations in the cabins of his partners he need carry nothing, s t o p p i n g when he pleased, staying as long as he pleased. He was a miner of miners. How he got his start or how he ended I don't know. He treated us well. The last I heard of King Alex was a newspaper report he had gone to England and married a titled lady.

One day after the ice had gone out and transportation was over the muddy trails along the streams, I saw several horses going down the trail tied halter and tail. There were four men in charge, one man leading the string, a man on either side, and a fourth man bringing up the rear.

I was interested because there had been only one horse in the Dawson country all winter so far as I knew. I presume these came in by boat after the ice went out. I inquired what the horses meant; they had small packs on their backs. I was told that it was McDonald's first shipment of gold to Dawson after the cleanup and the horses were carrying seven hundred and fifty pounds of gold, or about one hundred and fifty thousand dollars worth.

* * * * *

Alex's hiking over his circuit illustrates how indifferent men were about taking long trips on foot that winter over broken trails. I was in a lodging house in Dawson one night in December and overheard one man say to another, "What are you going to do tomorrow, Bill?"

"Why, I'm going over to Sulphur and Dominion. Better come along."

"Well, I don't know but I will; I have nothing else to do." Just that casual. Now that meant about one hundred and thirty miles one way, carrying blankets and grub, in winter weather, possibly camping out more or less. It was amazing!

* * * * *

Then there was George W. Carmack, who, with his two Indian brothers-in-law, made the first discovery. George staked Discovery claim, which was double in size, and his brothers-in-law staked No. 1 above and No. 1 below, giving the three two thousand feet up and down the creek.

They worked a large number of men, and one day toward spring I went up to see if he could give me a job. There were two little breed children coasting down the creek bank near his cabin. They were cluck-clucking their funny language to each other and were so busy they didn't notice me as I stood observing them several minutes. I asked them which cabin was Carmack's. They both pointed to a certain cabin. As I approached the cabin, I heard the drone of an old fashioned melodeon. I had to knock several times before I attracted attention, then the melodeon stopped. When the door opened, there stood an old squaw—they looked old prematurely. I asked to see Carmack.

She came out to the corner of the cabin and pointed to another cabin farther up and across the creek. Apparently she spoke no English for the only sound she made was "EEEEE" as she pointed. That was Carmack's wife. I thanked her and went over to the other cabin, a bare room containing only a stove and water tub, in which Carmack was swirling a gold pan. As I darkened the door, which was open, he looked up, rather a spare man of perhaps fifty years, black piercing eyes, and clipped beard three or four inches long.

In answer to my question, he shook his head and remarked, "Season is about over. Am letting the men go."

* * * * *

It wasn't always necessary to sink holes to bed-rock in working a claim. That was generally so, but occasionally the bed-rock cropped out at the surface, necessitating a different procedure. Our friends Fuller and Brown had one of these crop-out claims. A long bend of Bonanza left a peninsular-shaped bench opposite No. 6 below Bonanza. This bench was a pushed-up, ragged bed-rock. Here it was unnecessary to sink holes. Fuller and Brown had staked this bench, built a fine cabin, and made themselves comfortable. The interesting thing about their claim was that it could be worked more cheaply during the summer than in the winter. They had made themselves comfortable all winter and waited for the sun to come back to them and their diggings.

When the sun returned in the spring, cleared the snow off and thawed the roughened surface, they set up a rocker and rocked out from fifteen to twenty dollars in two to three hours. Where convenient, sluice boxes were run across such claims, speeding up the work considerably.

* * * * *

Toward spring, as the season for sluice boxes and flumes approached, there was a general run around to secure nails offering as much as five dollars a pound, but nails were very scarce. As a result, many boxes were fastened together by wooden pegs. The ingenuity of these gold hunters was a continual surprise. One could not enter a cabin anywhere without seeing some ingenious gadget.

* * * * *

A whole chapter might be written about windows. The common glass window of the outside was not to be had for all those cabins, and all kinds of substitutes were used. The most common were made of bottles, but where the bottles came from one could only guess. The frame was made with counter sunk places for the bottom of the bottles at top and bottom; the bottom row of bottles standing upright, and the top row, necks down. The necks met in a hole bored in an inch strip across the middle of the frame. Then the open spaces between bottle and shoulder and middle strip were stuffed with moss. This made a window with two rows of bottles. Quite a few had the greased muslin window such as we had. A very few had windows made of real window glass only of odd shaped pieces. It seemed some had attempted to bring in window panes only to have them broken, but they had saved the pieces.

Every cabin had a small balance scale for weighing gold, and much ingenuity had been employed to mount those balances. The scale was originally constructed to be held up by a ring with one hand, while the weights and gold were manipulated with the other hand, but nearly every cabin had a different mount for balancing those scales. There were also many crooked ways of weighing, one might weigh honestly or cheat as desired. Necessity was the mother of invention, but sometimes the daddy was the devil.

* * * * *

I have often been asked if Indians didn't have an odor. I would say, generally speaking, all people have, but different skins throw off different odors, some stronger than others. The Indian has an odor, which may come from being continually smoked around open fires and uncleanliness. I remember on several occasions, on entering cabins, I asked, "Where is the Indian?"

"What Indian?" they would ask, of course.

"Well, the squaw you harbored last night."

They would laugh it off, but there was no mistaking the odor.

ODDS AND ENDS

I have just been reading the Lewis and Clark Journal, the fourth time I have read of that thrilling trip. There was one occurence of that trip which still interests me, I presume, because no plausible explanation was given. The Indians at Mandan told of strange sounds of the mountains which sounded like large guns in the distance, referring to the mountains beyond the Great Falls of the Missouri. Lewis and Clark mentioned hearing these sounds on several occasions but gave no reasonable explanation of their cause. Now I venture a theory since I have not learned the real cause.

My theory is that large boulders were rolled over water falls, or large segments were broken from the lip of the falls by the force of the spring freshet and chugged onto other boulders at the foot of the falls. The concussion from the striking boulders, coming from beneath the water, produces sounds like distant or muffled large guns.

I base my theory on our experience on Adams Creek. After the ice left the creek and the water was high and swift, we were puzzled for some time by strange muffled sounds like distant guns. We heard the sounds more distinctly at night and especially when our ear was to the pillow. We finally discovered it to be caused by large boulders rolling down the creek before the strong current and thumping into other boulders. They sometimes came singly and sometimes in a barrage.

* * * * *

One Sunday about a dozen of us congregated at one of the cabins up the creek to have a little visit. We were sitting mostly on the floor around the walls of the cabin, each one telling what he would do when he went "out." At these gatherings we nearly always talked about something to eat. One of the boys exclaimed, "When I get back home my wife will have to keep me supplied with sour-dough cakes!"

Another said, "And mine will have to bake my beans just like Popper bakes them here."

A dry, wise owl over in the corner said, with great dignity, "Yes-siree! and when I get home my wife will put on the table whatever she damn pleases, and I'll like it."

* * * * *

I must not forget to mention the Aurora Borealis, most beautiful there of any place in the world, I believe. The waves were more plentiful toward spring. We would go out nights to look at them. Nearly every night, we had those that met in a dome overhead, sending down streamers from a point overhead to the h o r i z o n all around, the streamers quivering and shooting their entire length. It seemed like the southernmost streamers might be those seen some nights in the northern states. In addition to the dome lights, we would have occasional lights like broad flags of rainbow colors, hanging on edge, come out over the top of one mountain and go waving in quick waves across the sky, from north to south, and disappear behind another mountain. I had read of these convolutions in the flag lights making a crackling noise as the waves ran across this long flag-like ribbon; and at times we thought we heard a kind of snapping, but we were never sure.

* * * * *

How Swiftwater and his partner got their rich location on Eldorado Creek, as reported, was interesting. Eldorado creek had a much shallower valley than other creeks, and old-timers thought it of no value because of this, and called it "The Cow Pasture." It was not staked till all of Bonanza creek had been staked. No prospecting had been done on Eldorado when Swiftwater and his partner came along, as poor as Job's turkey, and took a lay on No. 13. A report said that two Irishmen had refused a lay on No. 13 because of its unlucky number.

Swiftwater and partner began to sink a hole. Two more men came along and took a lay and began to sink. They sank four holes on each lay across the valley and reported ten and fifteen cents a pan. But they found how rich the claim really was and the last thing they did in each hole at bed-rock was to build a big fire and bring down the sides. These four men had jointly kept secret the fabulous wealth of the claim, and entered into a dicker with the owner to buy.

They finally bought the claim for forty thousand dollars, to be paid off from the first dirt to be washed. After getting the papers fixed up, those four men opened the old holes and paid the debt off in six weeks.

The first thirty-nine claims of Eldorado were said to produce from six to nine hundred thousand dollars per claim by the old hand method.

Another interesting incident regarding this creek was related to us. An old prospector came up the Bonanza and found two young friends in a cabin on Bonanza near the mouth of Eldorado. He stayed over night with these friends and the next day went on up to the head of Bonanza. On his return he reported all Bonanza staked and could not get a claim. His friends said, "Say, Oldtimer, we have two claims over on 'The Cow Pasture.' Don't think they are much good, but it was all we could get when we came up. Tell you what we'll do, we'll give you a deed to a third interest."

"No, I don't want it, there is nothing in that shallow valley."

"Well," they said, "we will make you a deed and when you go to Dawson, you have it recorded."

They got a piece of paper and made him a deed, and he went off down to Dawson, not intending to come back. When the news came out about the great wealth of the Eldorado, he found himself owner of a third interest in two of the richest claims in the Klondike.

XIX

SCURVY!

We put in some time reading aloud, as we had gotten hold of some books somewhere. First one would read awhile, then the other. Then we shot mice and mosquitoes, and practiced making flapjacks. In this last accomplishment we wished to excel and turn them like sourdoughs should. Take hold of the pan handle, give the jack a little flip and it turns over. By much practice, the jacks will nearly turn of their own accord.

We had lots of fun learning. The cook at the time would take hold of the pan, get in the middle of the floor, shake the cake loose a little, then heave it into the air. We used to throw them five or six feet high until we got control of the thing. When it came down we would try to catch it in the pan, but often it landed squarely on the edge of the pan and cut the cake in two, half going on the floor or wrapping itself around the side of the pan.

Did we actually shoot mice and mosquitoes? We tried to, anyway. Little red mice with short tails inhabited the cabin with us. We thought we had the better right, and while lying in our hammocks, we would practice shooting our revolvers at them. It made a terrible noise indoors, and we got diversion from it.

About the mosquitoes, there were two kinds up there. A very large one, standing about a half-inch high, and a small one, smaller than those in the States. The large ones were not bad, but the small ones were surely hot numbers.

I never saw the big ones they told about. These stood straddle of the Yukon and speared the sourdoughs out of their boats as they passed down stream between the mosquitoes' legs. I am inclined to think that story came from the Paul Bunyan camp.

But we actually did shoot at the large ones we saw. We had a ventilator up in the gable, and when the sun went down in the spring, the large 'skeeters' would perch along the edge of that box to get the warmth that came up from below, I suppose. We could see them against the sky from our bunks. We got to shooting them like a couple of kids, "Now see that one an inch from the corner? I'll take him." Bang! An awful report, and dust showered down from the box.

By the first of May Duncan was ailing. He had been feeling unfit for some time, but now we discovered he had the dreaded scurvy. Dreaded when there was no remedy at hand. The scurvy is caused by lack of vegetable foods, a thickening of the blood that prevents it from circulating freely through the capillary veins, the farthest extremities from the heart being the first affected. The large tendon back of the heel, Tendon of Achilles, is the first to become affected.

Duncan's tendons became sore and seemed like to break when he walked. Then the cords back of the knees got sore and stiff. He had a hard time trying to get around. The skin on his ankles and up to the knees got yellow in irregular splotches, about two inches in size. Then these splotches turned darker until they were the color of liver. In the final stages, this part of the body begins to rot off.

There was a lot of this sickness up and down the creeks at that time. Forty men had died of it in the Dawson hospital up to the present time. There were some doctors and many would-be doctors and some medicine in Dawson, but no fresh vegetables, so the poor fellows died. A few fresh potatoes would have saved many lives.

A man who worked on the windlass next to Judge Osborne all winter had died. We had seen him every day there at work, and had inquired about him, only to learn he had gone to the hospital with scurvy and later had died. He was perhaps fifty years old, wore a full beard about six inches long. I can see him now, day after day winding that windlass, and, I suppose, thinking of his loved ones at home and what he would do for them when he cleaned up his million. He never went home. I didn't know his name.

We went to work with every sourdough remedy mentioned to save Duncan. The most common remedy was spruce tea, made by boiling spruce needles. He drank gallons of that bitter stuff to no purpose, and no other thing we could find did him any good. He got rapidly worse. It was surely getting serious.

Two old-timers, A. D. Fuller and Reuben Brown, on a bench claim down below, came up one Sunday and said, "We are going to Dawson, what can we bring you?"

We said, "Irish potatoes, if you can get them, or anything else you can find for this scurvy."

"What shall we pay for them?" they asked.

"Give them the whole sack!" we answered.

The ice had gone out of the small creeks, and the sun was making the snow disappear on the mountain tops, so they had a bad trail to Dawson and did not get back for several days. They brought nothing for us from Dawson but bad news.

Duncan got out of the cabin at first, slowly and with short steps, then by the aid of a stick, then on his knees, then rolled out. Finally, he couldn't get out at all. I made a bunk for him on the floor. I frantically ransacked the cabins up and down the gulches for miles every day to find anything available to stop scurvy. I got a little vinegar, a few pickles, but mostly remedies. It seemed hopeless. I sat nights by the fire with my head in my hands, wondering about his death in all its ramifications. And what should I do with him when he died. I finally planned to make a box for him and bury him in the prospect hole we had sunk behind the cabin. There he would be frozen for all time and could be taken home any time, if desired. Of course, we did not talk of death.

I had been down Bonanza several hours one day. I had gone farther than usual and had found several little things recommended. I stewed up a tomato can full of spruce tea and another can full of other dope and placed them before him on the floor before I left, telling him, "There is your medicine." He had always taken everything I fixed for him without protest. He said nothing in protest then, and I went down the Bonanza.

It was late afternoon when I returned, and I got a shock. As I entered the cabin, he was lying with his face to the wall and did not greet me, which was unusual. I walked over to him, thinking he was dead. My heart seemed to be standing still; I was dizzy. I noticed his cans had not been touched; they were full as I had left them. But he was breathing and awake. He had given up.

The rebound of my heart made me tingle. I lost my head, or did I? I have never been able to decide. I threw my hat against the wall with a bang, and did what I had never dared do in our lives before. I cussed him up and down. "You blankety blank, blank. I run my legs off up and down the face of the whole earth to find you medicine, and you lie there and don't take it!"

I didn't fly off through anger, but fright. I was frozen stiff with fright to see him give up. He wasn't an easy quitter, and I feared the worst had come. He knew exactly why and how I felt and saw the funny side of my conduct. He rolled over with a big grin on his face and said, "Give me that damn stuff!" I pushed it at him, and, holding that wonderful grin, he gulped it down.

I told him of all the wonderful cures? I had found, and he seemed to cheer up a little.

The next day was Sunday, and Fuller and Brown came up again. They proposed to get a number of men and carry him down to the hospital. This was a monumental task over the mud trail at that time and showed the big hearts of those men.

Duncan looked at them a while then said, "If I must die, I'll die right here. The hospital at Dawson is full of scurvy cases, and they can do nothing for them; they are dying every day."

Fuller and Brown knew the truth of this, and also, the gravity of the situation. They stayed several hours, and, bless their hearts, they hatched an idea that was worth all the gold in the Klondike.

"Listen!" one of them said. "THE SOUR DOCK AND PEPPER WEEDS"—I capitalize them—"must be coming through the moss up on the mountain where the snow melted first."

"That's right," the other said. Then turning to me, "Do you know those weeds?"

I said I did not.

"Then I'll tell you what to do; you come down to our cabin in the morning, and one of us will go up the hill with you and see if we can find them."

I was there at sun-up, and we went up the side of the mountain and found two kinds of little shoots about two inches high, bearing a couple of leaves about one half inch long at the top of the stems. The stems were not as thick as a knitting needle.

We pulled gently upward on them, and there came up, attached, white, straight, single-stemmed roots, four or five inches long. They broke off down there where the thawed moss met the frost.

He said, "These things will grow rapidly now they have started, and in a few days you will be able to get a lot of them; especially on your side of the valley, where the sun has been hitting the longest. You get them and stew them like greens, which they are, and salt them to taste."

I went up our hill in the afternoon and found them; and after much careful labor, I got about a pint of them. I cooked them as directed and gave them to Duncan. The aroma made him wild. He gulped them down like a starved coyote, drank every drop of the liquid, and said it was the best stuff he had ever tasted in his life.

I continued, day by day, to get the weeds, and every day I found them longer and with more leaves on the stems. In about a week, I could grasp quite a number at one time.

SCURVY!

I got more and more each time, till one day I came down with a six-quart pail full. I set it on the stove and poured water on to cover it. The pail was full to the top. I seasoned it, and when it was cooked, I gave it to him right in the pail. He cleaned out that pail, believe it or not!

And from the time Duncan began on those weeds, he began to improve. In two weeks he got up on his feet and groped around the cabin walls, and on the fourth of June he walked eight miles down the trail toward Dawson. Those old-timers and the weeds saved his life, without a doubt.

We decided, when Duncan got his strength back and the season was more advanced, we would go out. We would go back home and leave that country to whom it might concern.

XX

HOMEWARD BOUND

By the first of June, Duncan felt we could move any time, as he was getting stronger every day. We called on our friends to say good-bye. Kincaid said, "What are you going to do with your rifle?"

"We are going to leave everything just as it is, except our blankets and a little grub," I said. "You can go up any time and get the rifle. We leave on the fourth."

He said, "I'll not take it for nothing, I'll give you ten dollars for it." He weighed out ten dollars and gave it to me. Fuller and Brown insisted on giving me twenty dollars and a nugget for each of my children, for the rest of the stuff. There are thoughtful people everywhere.

We thought we might get a small boat and navigate the lower Yukon to St. Michaels, but everyone advised against it. It was too long a trip, that eighteen hundred and fifty miles to Michaels. We could never make it.

We left the cabin the morning of the fourth of June and walked eight miles down Bonanza, Duncan with a cane, and I with a pack. A friend had told us to stop at a certain claim and stay over night with some friends of his; and, also, he had a cabin up a certain street in Dawson which we were to use as long as we wanted to. He gave us the key and told us where to leave it when we got through with it. Duncan made the eight miles like a top.

We were made welcome at the eight-mile stop and stayed over night.

There were three men in partnership on that lay. They had washed out about seven thousand dollars; half was to go to the owner. They did not get rich. One wanted to get enough to buy a farm in Oklahoma. That may have been the first cause of my going to Oklahoma eight years later.

134

I had a long pocket knife, one of those with a fawn foot for a handle and a five or six-inch blade. One of the boys saw me using it and became excited. "There is the very knife I have been wanting for years!" he exclaimed.

I passed it over to him saying, "I would give it to you only it is no good; I was going to throw it away. It would be just the thing, but it has poor stuff in the blade; it won't keep an edge."

He said, "What will you take for it?"

I said, "Keep it."

"No, I won't do that," he said. "How many children did you say you had?"

When I told him I had two children, he got two nuggets and gave them to me against my protest.

On the fifth, we reached Dawson in good shape, found the cabin, and made ourselves at home. There were no furnishings but a stove; it was fine anyway. The next day I went down along the city front. The ice was all out of the Yukon, and about two miles of boats of all kinds were tied to the shore, their sides touching each other. It was estimated that nearly thirty thousand new-comers had followed the ice down in those boats.

I was walking along the river bank about the center of Dawson's front and saw a big barge tied to shore bearing a sign, "Irish potatoes, $1.00 per pound." I asked the owner how many he had, and he said, "About a ton."

I said, "Gee, you've got a stake right there. You can get more than $1.00 per pound!"

He said, "Yes, I know. See that sign in front of that building? I sold him a sack this morning." I looked to where he was pointing and saw a sign, "Irish Potatoes, $3.60 per pound."

"But," said the barge man, "I shall not sell for more than $1.00 per pound and no more than a sack to any one person. The hospital is full of scurvy, and they are needed up there to save those boys' lives."

"You are a new kind of man. One doesn't see your kind of man every day."

135

He laughed, and said, "A dollar a pound will pay me well, and I will be satisfied with that."

"How the Sam Hill did you get them over the pass in winter and down here in good condition?" I asked.

"Well, we had to fight for it, that's the truth," he said.

"But they are in fine shape. Just look at them!" I told him I had a partner just getting over the scurvy and I would like five or six pounds for him. He weighed me out six pounds, and I bought a little fresh meat farther up.

Now we were to decide how we were to go out. Everyone here, too, said, "Oh, you can't go to Michaels in a small boat." There were two large river steamers tied up at Dawson that had come up since the ice went out. We went down next day, the seventh, to see about them. They didn't know when they would discharge their cargoes, and the fare to Michaels was one hundred and fifty dollars, and from there to Seattle another one hundred and fifty dollars.

We decided that would not do. We would neither wait nor pay the price. We went up along the shore, looking at the boats tied up all along, and found a great variety to choose from and suspected we might buy any one of them, if desired.

We found a thirty-foot boat that we thought might make the trip. It had a forward deck of about six feet, a seven and a half-foot beam with mast, five oars and a sixteen-foot sweep. It had a three-foot side and was light and well built.

The next morning, we had decided to try to find the owner and get four more men, if possible. I went down to see what could be done. I was standing looking at the boat when a nice man, about fifty years old, came along. He asked if the boat belonged to me. I said "No, but I wish it did."

"What would you do with it?" he asked.

"I would go to Michaels in it," I answered.

"Say! Any chance to go along?" he asked excitedly.

"There might be, I would have to see my partner."

Then followed many questions back and forth. As we were talking, along came a man about thirty-five years old. I asked him if he knew to whom the boat belonged. He said it belonged to him.

"Do you want to sell it?"

"I don't know, I may need it."

"What for, you going to Michaels?"

"No. I just came in and am going to stay awhile anyway."

"Well, the boat is no use to you in here; you can't get it up any of the creeks. It is good for only one thing: to go down the river, unless you want to make a chicken house of it." He laughed, and after asking a number of questions, said he would sell for thirty dollars. I told him to come on down to the bunkhouse and I would weigh out his money. He looked at me quizzically and asked, "Weigh out the money?"

I said, "Yes."

He laughed. "Never heard of such a thing. 'Weigh out the money.' What do you mean?"

I said, "The only money in here is gold and it must be weighed."

"How will I know I get my thirty dollars?"

"We'll let the hotel man weigh it."

"O. K. Let's go."

He had never seen gold in its natural state and was interested. We went down to the bunk-house and the other man went along. I gave my sack to the manager and said, "Weigh out thirty dollars for this man."

He put the weights in one pan, then poured out the thirty dollars, and said, as he turned away, "There is your thirty dollars."

The man looked at it and laughed heartily. "Now what shall I do with it," he asked.

"Got a sack?" I asked.

"No, I haven't," he answered.

"Then wrap it up good in a piece of paper and put it where it won't get away from you. It slides very easily." He got a piece of paper and had a lot of fun stowing away his first gold. I wrote a receipt in my note book and he signed it, "N. G. Patterson."

My new friend told me his name was Brown, from Waterloo, Iowa. He had been a manufacturer of brooms, had been in the Klondike all winter, and was ready to go out. We went up the front street together, and, when we came to the street our cabin was on which ran up the hill at right angles to Front or Main street, I stopped, and wrote on a leaf of my note book:

Dawson, June 8th, 1898.
Wanted: Four men to join two others in a small
boat to Michaels. Second cabin from the last
on the right side of this street.

I tore out the leaf, found a stick, and posted it at the corner. We went on up to the cabin, and I introduced Brown to Duncan. We were glad to accept Brown as the third man, and he was equally pleased to join us. We all sat on the floor as there were no chairs. In about five minutes there came a rap.

"Is this the place four men are wanted to go to Michaels?"

"Yes, come in." A big fellow by the name of Vochs, a telegrapher from Wisconsin, came in. Five minutes later another man came in, a clothing merchant from Chicago, Lorenz, by name. He had been in only three weeks. In another five minutes there came Dave Hetherington from Seattle. He had been in all winter. Vochs had also been in all winter. Dave had no particular calling outside. Just worked around at anything, summers, and hunted bears on Kodiak Island in winter. Right on Dave's heels came another man. We had to tell him we were full up and asked him to destroy the notice as he went down by the corner, to stop others.

Could we reach Michaels? All these men were willing to try it with us. We only needed organizing.

138

How many more there were in Dawson who wanted to go down in a small boat is not known, but likely there were many, as it took us so short a time to get our quota.

We made a list of our belongings, figured how much more we would need for thirty days or six weeks, and appointed a committee to get supplies. All were to get credit for what they had, and we were to pay equally. We had it all lined up in short order and expected to get away the eleventh. They all left but Vochs and Brown, and we visited for a time. In the midst of our talk, Vochs remarked that he liked the appearance of all but Dave. Dave was thirty-eight years old, bald, sandy complexioned, and spoke in a high, thin voice. He was about one hundred and fifty pounds in weight. Well, "One can't tell how far a frog will jump by just looking at him." I want to say that Dave proved the best all round man in the bunch.

While we are waiting for the other men to come back with their outfits, I'll tell you a funny story.

As we were enroute to Dawson the fifth of June, we saw a funny thing. We reached the Klondike river about where the winter portage left that stream and crossed over to the Bonanza. There we found a foot-bridge had been built over the Klondike, planks laid lengthwise reaching from one pair of legs to another pair and a guide rail three feet high to steady one. The stream was perhaps two hundred yards wide at that point, but shallow.

As we reached the forward end of the bridge, we turned to take a look back and up and down the stream and were amazed to see a man coming down the middle of the stream, sitting on the top of the water. "Now, what do you know about that?" one of us said. He was coming quite swiftly, as the current was good, and he was stroking the water first on one side then on the other with a stick four feet long. Laughing, we called to him, "Where are you from?"

"All the way from Hunker Creek. I'm old man Hunker himself," all in a broad Irish brogue.

We looked at him. His feet and hips were in the water—and that water was cold—and around his hips a few ends of willows stuck up. That was all, but he was making good time and seemed to enjoy it.

He had made a light raft of some kind on which to drift down stream and found, when he got his weight upon it, he was just too heavy; but, not to be beat, he had suffered part of his anatomy to contact the water rather than pull to shore and add more timber to the raft. Of such stuff are prospectors made.

XXI

GOODBYE, DAWSON

Dawson was a very orderly mining camp. In this respect, much different from the gold fields of the States in the past. In the mining camps of the States the miners had to organize their own governments. And usually they put if off until the depredations of road agents compelled action and necessitated a lot of hanging and shooting.

Dawson was different. The Canadian Government sent a judge and a bunch of Mounties in there early. Those officials always meant business. A certain amount of wine, women, and gambling was over-looked, but robbery and murder were practically unknown.

On our trip to Michaels, we were to be favored with sunlight all the time—either twilight or direct sunlight. A short twilight at midnight and long sunlight covered the whole twenty-four hours. We calculated the "Twilight Belt" had passed over that district by the middle of April, but at midnight, April, fifteenth, we could not distinguish it. We found, however, a strong twilight at midnight May, fifteenth, and it would be strong till the end of July. So we proposed to run the full twenty-four hours.

In outfitting the boat, we bought a bill of goods which shows the difference in prices in June, '98, compared with prices the previous winter. Here it is:

10 lbs. beans	$ 3.00
3 cans milk	3.00
10 lbs. potatoes	8.50
20 lbs. dried fruit	9.00
30 lbs. sugar	22.00
3 lbs. coffee	3.00
40 lbs. bacon	16.00
2 sacks flour	14.00
10 lbs. rolled oats	4.00

141

KLONDIKE DIARY

There had been a considerable drop in the prices since I bought in February.

Our whole expense, counting boat and equipment, was $148.50, about $25.00 each. Compared with the $900.00 the steamboats wanted to land us at Michaels the difference was worth trying for.

We decided that if we found we could not make Michaels on our own, for any reason, we would hail a down going steamer and go on board. What they would charge us in that case was questionable.

We had been away from home about a year and had no word from the folks till we came to Dawson on the fifth of June. Then we got all the mail that had been following us for that time. The Canadian mail had not moved all winter. There was reported to be nine tons held at the pass. It came down after the ice, and we got ours in a bunch. Some of the news was good and some very bad. Our father had passed away in November, grieving for us. Among the mail was a photograph of my wife and one each of the two little tykes. What a joy they brought me!

When I was in Dawson in February, I had caught the U. S. mail carrier and sent a letter by him, which was the first they had received since the one I had sent out by Swiftwater in October. The folks got the Swiftwater letter in December. The envelope I had put it in had worn to fragments in his pocket and he had placed it in a new envelope at Seattle. The men had made good time.

I should say a word about the U. S. mail carriers on the Yukon. In fact, one could not give them too much praise; they were unsung heroes. I had been proud, and still am proud, to have met one of them and sent a letter by him from Dawson in February. Those young men had a route from Dyea to Circle City, one thousand miles, and they made the trip one way, singly, each month, passing each other on the way. One lone man with two dogs, pulling the mail and necessary outfit one thousand miles over that trail in winter, was an heroic task. And, so far as I have learned, they never fell down on the job.

We were all set to leave Dawson for Michaels the 11th of June; and at ten-thirty-five o'clock a.m., shoved off on our eighteen hundred and fifty mile trip. We had no misgivings. We had our duffle thrown about the boat in confusion; but with better than a six mile current, we just deported ourselves about the boat, getting better acquainted, and let the current take us as it chose. Prow first, stern first, side-wise, we let it drift. Soon Dawson passed from sight, and we bid it good-bye.

At noon we came to a good landing place where there was lots of wood and we ran in. While some of us arranged the boat for convenience and comfort, others put on a supply of wood for the stove, and others cooked our dinner. We could all cook better or worse, but as Dave and Lorenz were best, they fell into that job naturally.

We stowed wood up under the front deck all ready for the stove. Dave had his head with him and had provided some boards and a box, the use of which had puzzled me, but I had said nothing about them. Now I was to see a piece of ingenuity. He cut the two boards long enough to fit crosswise of the boat close to the front deck and nailed them in place so they would let the box fit between them. He nailed the box in the middle between these boards which were on edge. The box was about eight inches in depth. He then put about three inches of sand in the bottom of the box and placed the stove on the sand. He had measured that box in Dawson, no doubt, for the stove just fit with a couple of inches all around to spare. Into this space he poured sand, then wired the stove to the sides of the boat, stuck in three joints of pipe, and had a stove that would not fire the boat and still would ride solidly in all kinds of rough water.

The other boys hung the cooking utensils about the sides of the boat on nails, handy to be reached by the cook, and stowed the grub under the beam where he could get it handily. The whole front of the mast was made into a kitchen, and such a kitchen any housewife might be satisfied with.

We others brought in two poles seven feet long and two, five feet long, and lashed their ends together, making a frame on the boat bottom back of the rowers' benches. We filled this frame with small spruce boughs six or eight inches deep, on which we spread a canvas, and had a bed three men could sleep in comfortably, and had room along the sides for others to pass by. There was still lots of room at the stern for the man on the sweep to move about. I'll say we were comfortable in that boat.

After eating a good dinner, we shoved off. The current took us on its loving bosom and ran us out to midstream, where it playfully whirled us about. We let it whirl. We had all passed through much hardship and were disposed to rest in laziness.

We let it drift with the current, while we swapped yarns. At nine o'clock p.m., we divided ourselves into two shifts of three men each, three for the night and three for the day, but we had no darkness. Lorenz, Vochs and Brown took the day shift and turned in for the night. Duncan, Dave and I were on night duty.

At ten o'clock p. m., we reached Forty-mile, a camp on the left bank of the Yukon. We landed and left a letter for the folks back home, to be given to the U. S. carrier on his trip out. The boys there were out of sugar, and we traded them some. As we drifted away, they shouted, "What's taking you out?"

We called back, "We're going out to fight the Spaniards."

"Hurrah, hurrah, hurrah, we wish we were going with you!" they shouted after us.

It got chilly along about midnight, as the sun dipped behind the north hills, and we three pulled blankets about our shoulders to keep warm. My notes at this time say: "As I write this, it is between twelve and one o'clock a. m., and I can see quite clearly by the strong twilight.

At three a. m., we called the day watch, according to agreement, and we day men turned in. At six-thirty, I woke to hear the day men talking about a steamer on a sand bar. I turned out to find the steamer "Seattle No. I" high and dry. She had been aground nine days, and, as the river was falling, she showed more hull every day. It was, probably, her grave.

Here we got into the mosquitoes right. They had not been bad up the creeks for some reason. Had seen them bad in Illinois. But now we were to get acquainted in earnest. We sewed mosquito netting around the rims of our hats and fastened it to our coats. We put on our gloves. This was fine so long as we didn't have to move around much and dislodge the netting. These pests circled our heads in a broad black belt. To see each other, we had to duck or raise our heads quickly to catch a momentary glimpse of each other. And what a singing!

We landed at Circle City at ten a. m., the thirteenth. Just twenty-five minutes less than forty-eight hours from Dawson, or three hundred miles. Hadn't used oar nor sail. Counting off lost hours, we had drifted nearly seven miles per hour. We walked around Circle a while and shopped. Found it more like a city than Dawson, older, of course.

The steamer "Hamilton" was tied up there and almost ready to pull out for Dawson. At eleven a. m., we left just as the steamer "Bella" came in, minus her barge, which she was obliged to leave some miles down the river, and which we passed later. My note: "The afternoon passed pleasantly away as we drifted along amidst green islands and the songs of birds, the scent of the Balm-of-Gilead and spring in the air."

Toward evening, we were struck by a strong wind from the north, and as we were traveling north-west, it drove us south, among the many islands, the Yukon here being five to six miles wide and full of islands.

In the lee of the islands, we were protected from the wind and thought it a good time to lay in a lot of fine wood, as nearly all the islands had considerable drift wood stacked up on their upper ends.

We pulled into a pile of drift wood, and three of us jumped off and began chopping and sawing. But zowie! Our netting would fly up with our motions and the enemy would make a grand assault. They filled our eyes, mouths, and nostrils. They routed us completely. You never saw such persistent "skeeters." They landed and crawled and bit. I pulled off my gloves to see what they would do. They landed so thick I could not see my hands.

I stroked one hand with the other and brought off my finger tips ropes of crushed mosquitoes, and could continue doing that, it looked like, forever. They crawled up our sleeves and down our shirts like crazy bedbugs. They did not bite through the clothing. They got inside and crawled and bit till they were crushed. We scrambled on board and ran away as if a hundred swarms of bees were after us. We rowed out to the main stream to the north where the strong wind could strike us and blow the pests away. We found a gravel bar extending out quite a distance into the stream where the wind struck us with force, and we pulled up on it to wait till the wind went down.

It was ten-thirty p. m., the thirteenth of June, and we were above the Arctic Circle. We wished it were nearer the twenty-third so we might see the midnight sun. Duncan and I decided to wait up and see what the sun would do. The others lay down to sleep after warning us to wake them at twelve o'clock to see also.

I had noticed a moose track on the bar and got a shotgun—we had two along—and some buck shot shells and struck into the timber. But the enemy was waiting, the branches caught my netting, and I was driven back.

Duncan was rigging up some fishing tackle and I joined him. For an hour we tried it but gave it up. It was approaching twelve o'clock, and the sun was still in full view so we called the boys. We all watched the sun; it touched the hill tops far to the north, sank slowly down to its middle, and then, glory be, it rose and went sailing away off up to the right, to make its twenty-four hour circle again. We had seen the midnight sun and were happy. As there is considerable stretch of the Yukon above the Circle, we could have seen it again the next night but for some clouds on the north horizon.

We pulled out and, using five oars and the sweep, we battled the wind. It was little use; our boat caught too much wind. We pulled onto the next bare point, tied up and all turned in to sleep. I woke at six-thirty and found the day shift trying to fight the wind again. It was gradually subsiding. About noon, we came to Fort Yukon, a few log cabins and tents. We saw three white men and a lot of Indians there. We ate dinner and left at three p. m.

Along here, at a bend in the river, we saw, upon the left bank, what we took to be a settlement of log cabins. On our approach, we discovered the supposed cabins to be large blocks of ice that had been pushed up there as the ice went out on high water. The blocks were immense in size, even larger than cabins when we got close to them. I do not know how thick the ice gets on the Yukon, but those blocks were amazing. We saw another apparent settlement but waited to see if it were houses or ice. It was ice.

Again we saw this phenomenon, and one of the boys said, "Can't fool me this time. That is a town." We all agreed, but it was ice. As the ice thawed out, the sand and dirt it contained stuck to the surface and gave the blocks a black color, and was, at a distance, the color and shape of log cabins.

June fourteenth we were off for Fort Hamlin. For two nights and a day we had a good wind down stream. Up went our ten foot square sail and away we went. With the sail pulling and the current pushing, we made good time. It rained a little, the first rain we had seen since leaving Lake Bennett in October.

147

KLONDIKE DIARY

We arrived at Fort Hamlin at eight o'clock a. m., Thursday after a good run of two hundred and forty miles from Fort Yukon. Hamlin had one log store and a few tents, one white man and a lot of Indians. The white man was the store-keeper and was still in bed. We needed some items of food and woke him up. We looked around his almost empty store but found nothing we needed.

Our next stop was Minouk, seventy-five miles below. We arrived there at one o'clock p. m., and found quite a settlement of whites and Indians. We made some purchases there, and a "Captain" of some sort showed me some samples of their gold. It looked good, and he wanted us to stop there and go mining.

We stopped a half hour at Minouk, or Minonk, then headed through the Rampart Narrows for Tanana. They told us we would have no trouble in the Narrows; we didn't, but what a beautiful current! As we approached the Rampart Mountains, the river had narrowed up, and it looked like we would run head on into the mountain or an underground river. One of my strongest impressions is that of entering the Ramparts.

XXII

OLD SOURDOUGH AND INDIANS

Friday morning, June seventeenth, at one-thirty, we passed a steamer going up, and another at four-thirty. We were unable to make out their names. They had strong current to buck and were going slowly, much slower than we on the down current. And how the smoke was belching from their funnels! We passed Tanana at noon, did not stop. We had a good wind and were whooping it up. By five o'clock, it had calmed. The sun shone down on us, and it got warm. The boys all went to sleep except Vochs and I, as we floated along on the current.

As night came on, no darkness of course, it became sultry, and the mosquitoes came after us in full force. Then came pulling toward us an old sourdough, in a small boat, all alone and suffering from the scurvy. He was a real character. He tied to us and drifted with us all night just to have some one to talk to. He was, perhaps, in his seventies, heavy set, bushy whiskers and hair.

We learned a valuable point from him. We told him about having trouble with head winds back at Fort Yukon, and he said, "Why didn't you put out your horses?"

"Horses—what do you mean?"

"Why, fill a sack with rocks and throw it overboard at the prow by a rope, and it will tote you right along."

"Well, that is a good one, we will remember it."

In the morning he left us with a "Good luck."

Later, in the head winds, we improved on the old man's idea. We filled two sacks with rocks, lashed boughs to the sacks, and threw one over each side of the prow. The current took hold of those boughs, the rocks held them down, and as the ropes stretched out in front, we had two horses, and away we went as fast as the current. Hurrah! No more trouble with head winds.

149

As we lay in our bunk on the bottom of the boat, we had all noticed a peculiar thing. With the ear down, we heard an unusual noise. We talked about it and wondered. It sounded like heavy sand or fine gravel grinding on the bottom of the boat. But it could not be that, for there was no sand showing in the water. It was several days before we solved the mystery. It was, undoubtedly, the gravel moving on the river bottom, being rolled along by the current and pieces of rock striking against each other. It was a continual grind, similar to rain on the roof but more of a metallic sound and could be heard only with an ear to the boat bottom.

We were running along one morning and saw what looked to be a birch bark canoe stuck end down in a pile of drift wood. It had, evidently, been carried down the stream with the wood and was piled up with it, at a bend in the river. We pulled over and extricated it from the wood. It was a beauty, and we decided to take it along. The owner would never find it anyway, and it would eventually be crushed with the wood.

Brother and I had a desire to take it back to Illinois as a souvenir.

We did not know how we could do it, but we would take it as far as possible, so we took it in tow.

Later in the day, as we were passing a high perpendicular point, against which the stream was washing, a canoe shot out before us from behind this point. It contained two Indian boys, about eight and ten years old. We were electrified by the daring and skill of those boys as they shot their canoe through that swift and turbulent water. They did not see us till they shot past us, and then they wheeled, looking at us all agape.

We spoke and made signs for them to come close. When they came near, we pointed to our canoe and tried to make them understand how we found it and asked them if they might know to whom it belonged. They finally got the idea and flew into a terrible excitement. Wheeling their canoe and shaking their fists at us, they shot into shore and disappeared into the forest. We expected some trouble, but that was the last we saw of them.

Saturday forenoon we had a down wind and kited right along. We passed the "Thomas Dwyer" going up. She was puffing her best and needed to. We exchanged a few words with her.

Sunday, the nineteenth, we reached Nulato. Here we traded the Indians out of a salmon. We had secured some large white fish from them back at Fort Yukon and had enjoyed them very much. Here we were getting into the salmon country.

The Indians erect four tall poles, sinking their bottom ends solidly in the ground, spacing them in a six or eight foot square. About six or eight feet from the ground they bind the poles with four others on which they lay a platform of poles. This platform is above the reach of the dogs and children. Then, above the platform, they run other poles about two or three feet apart. The squaws clean and hang the salmon on these upper poles to sun dry. The fish are opened up the front and left intact along the back. They are hung up with the inside to the sun. They make a fine red display and can be seen quite a distance.

The Indians fish with nets. These nets are of various lengths and eight to twelve feet wide on a guess. On the far upper corner of the net is fastened an inflated bladder, which keeps that corner afloat, while the other or near corner is held by the man in the canoe. The bottom of the net is heavily weighted to keep it in a vertical position. Being a double affair, there are really two nets, one of large mesh, and the other of fine mesh, placed together. The Indian puts his net in the canoe and paddles up stream a little ways, then lets the bladder end out into the water and pays the net out till it is all out but the corner he is holding. It hangs vertical in the stream and the large mesh is up stream, the smaller mesh on the down stream side. The two nets fit close together. As he drifts down stream, the salmon rush into or against the net, push the small meshed net through the large meshes which forms a sack of the smaller meshed net as it is pushed through one of the large meshes, and the fish is imprisoned in the sack. The fish are taken to the drying frame and tossed up on the platform, where the squaws take care of them.

Here at Nulato, we got some salmon, and we asked, "How much?" "Ooo tobac. Ooo salt."

We gave them a little tobacco and salt. I asked if one of them had a bow and arrows to sell.

A short, lame, young Indian said, "Me!" and went hurrying to his tent and brought a four foot bow and six arrows. It was just a plain, straight, smoothed off stick but had an interesting cord. The cord or string was made of the sinew from along the back bone of a caribou. A number of sinews were twisted together into a rope about three-sixteenths of an inch thick. The arrows were about twenty inches long with iron points wrapped by sinew, feathered neatly with eagle feathers split down the shank. I bought it for three dollars, and still have it.

One strapping young Indian took the bow by one end, placed the other end on the ground, and by a press down with the left hand and a twist of the right, he threw a half hitch of the cord on the upper end of the bow, making the cord taut and the bow slightly bent. He then placed an arrow on the cord and in a flash, sent it skipping along the ground forty or fifty yards. With a grunt of approval, he handed it to me. I was glad he hadn't shot the arrow into the air for we never would have found it.

We pushed off from Nulato, and, in the boat, I tried to take the half-hitch from the bow in the same manner in which the Indian had placed it there, but I could not even bend the bow with my left hand. Several of the boys tried it, but could not do any better than I could. I finally laid the bow against the side of the boat, placed my foot in the middle of the bow, bending it and permitting me to take the half-hitch off. What a laugh those Indians would have had could they have seen us fight that bow.

That Sunday night was very calm. The river had widened and, as the current was not swift, we took to rowing for the first time. During the night, a head wind came up, we threw out our horses and drifted. The water got very rough; and, as we bobbed along on the waves, an Indian came along side in a canoe, reached up and hung on to the side of our boat. He could not speak English, and I enjoyed grunting and making signs with him. He seemed to be amused also, and, as he was bound for Anvik, he drifted with us till noon.

I pulled from my pocket the photographs of my wife and children. I handed him my wife's picture. I think he had never seen a photograph before. I said, "My squaw."

He looked at it a moment then, "Eeeeeee, Eeeeeee, Eeeeeee, Eeeeeee!" a long time. He didn't get through with his "Eeee's" for a full five minutes. Then he handed it back to me, and I handed him the pictures of my little boy and girl and his "Eeee's" were repeated.

The waves became bad. They broke over the sides of his canoe. After considerable water had got into his boat, we signed for him to come into ours. But instead, he pulled a brand new Winchester rifle from the side of his canoe and handed it up to me. For a moment I did not get his intention, but finally I took the gun. The Indian grabbed his paddle and struck out for shore a half-mile or more away. I will never forget the sight. His little birch-bark shot through those waves like a living thing. Up and down, rolling and tossing, he reached the shore. He jumped out, pulled the canoe up on the gravel and dumped out the water. Then he slid it into the water again, sprang in and was on his way to join us, which he did, all in twenty-five minutes. He put up his hand for his gun and I gave it to him.

Soon we came to where a big flock of geese were feeding along the shore. He pointed to one of our shot-

153

guns hanging along the side of the boat and made motions to let him take one and he would go and shoot a goose. We pointed to his rifle and motioned for him to use that, thinking he could not get close enough to use a shot gun, but he shook his head. Along about noon he left us and disappeared around a point on shore. We thought perhaps he had landed to have a sleep till the storm went down, as we were pitching and rolling considerably. We did not see him again.

Tuesday morning, we reached Anvik. At least, the others did. I had asked them to wake me at Anvik, but I awoke myself just as we were leaving, and I was peeved. The view I got indicated quite a nice village at the head of a beautiful bay.

We had not only got onto that part of the river where the birch-bark canoe was used, but where the wild fowl were plentiful. Ducks of all kinds flew by us. One of the boys killed several ducks, and we had a big kettle of stewed duck which we enjoyed very much.

The wind rose, and the water got so rough we decided to lay up till night when it usually calmed down a little. We pulled into an Indian camp on the right shore. There were about a dozen tents. They came down to greet us, as usual. We asked if they had any fish.

One man about thirty-five, perhaps, with unmistakable negro blood, who spoke good English, said he had only one fish and didn't want to sell it. He had it on a piece of rope in the water, and what a beauty! A live King salman, weighing about thirty pounds.

A short time later, after conferring with his rather handsome wife, he came to us and said he would trade us half his fish for some food stuffs.

"All right, what will you have?" we asked.

"Two cups flour, some tea and sugar." We gave him good measure and he gave us half the fish.

He was probably half-Negro and half-Indian. His wife, neatly dressed in a clean calico dress, looked like she might be half-Indian and half-white. She had her hus-

154

band help her carry a box outside the tent. It looked like a carpenter's chest. She opened the top into two leaves or doors with legs to hold them level, converting the box into a table. Then she placed on the table, from inside the box, china cups, saucers, plates, knives and forks, and spoons. They conferred a little while and the man went to see an old couple making a canoe. I watched from a distance.

While he was there, the woman put a frying pan on the camp stove in the fore end of the tent and fried some bacon. She then made batter out of the flour we had traded to them and cooked flapjacks. She made tea in a little teapot and called the others, her husband and the old folks. They sat, two on either side of the table.

After the feast, the old folks went back to their canoe building. I went over to watch them. The old man was pleased to have me take an interest in their work, but no more pleased than I. It would have pleased me very much to have stayed till the whole canoe was done.

It was to be a birch-bark, and I learned for the first time that they were built bottom up. He had selected a level piece of ground and had driven neat sawed pegs vertically into the ground. These pegs were set in pairs the form of the upper or open side of the canoe if placed top down when finished. He had a pile of smoothed off sticks about four feet long and two by one-half inches wide and thick. Taking one of these sticks he lashed one end to a peg. Then he bent the stick up and over in a high bow, and lashed the other end to the opposite peg.

I got the idea. Each of these bows was to be a rib, and when all the pegs had their bows, all the ribs would be in place. Then, inscribing all the bows, just above the pegs, would be lashed the rim, and, beginning against the rim, the bark would be fitted up to the keel from both sides.

He had a stack of this bark near and some already bored with neat holes along the edges about two inches apart and three-fourth inch from the edge. All his work was so scientifically correct I was surprised and greatly interested.

He took two of the pieces of bark and fitted them together to show me how it was done. Then he took a piece of root fiber about three-sixteenths of an inch square, pushed one end through the holes in the bark and sewed the pieces edge to edge, drawing them tight. I could see that when the fiber dried, it would shrink and pull all the tighter. Then over these seams was smoothed a clear gum which dried hard. They probably got the gum from a pine of some kind.

I wondered where he got the fiber and soon saw it all. His squaw came out of the forest with a bundle of sticks over her shoulder. As she approached, I saw the sticks were butts of long roots, the other ends of which came trailing on the ground behind her. She threw them down, then picked up one and stripped the bark from it, squared off the butt end, and, taking her knife, marked off the butt into little squares. She pried one of the little square ends out about an inch, then catching the end in her teeth pushed the root away with her hands, and a foot or more of that fiber ripped right out of the root but did not break. Then taking the fiber in one hand and the root in the other, she simply ripped that fiber from its neighbors the full length of the long root. She started another fiber the same way, ripping it off, just like that. She was piling up sewing fiber faster than a dozen could use it, if they tried; and there I learned how the old Indians got their teeth worn down in front to the gums. They used them as pincers where ever needed.

Just then Dave was standing in the boat with our large stew kettle—a five gallon can—balanced on the edge of the boat. He called to me: "Here is a nice lot of duck gravy. I have no place to put it, and I don't like to throw it out." I suggested the old squaw might like it.

Dave yelled to her. No response. He yelled again, and she looked up. He waved, pointing to the can.

She didn't seem much interested, but at his continued gesticulations, she came down, and he said, "You want?" pointing into the can.

She grabbed one edge of the can with a grimy paw, stuck the other into the gravy and put it to her mouth to taste.

"Ooooo!" She went scrambling up to her tent licking her paw and returned with a vessel to put the gravy in. She poured in what would run, then scraped the can clean with her other paw. Clean dirt, of course, never killed anyone, and that gravy full of duck meat was a treat.

XXIII

SWAMP AND INDIAN TROUBLE

Dave made us a good supper. He took that half salmon, cut off a piece the length of a bread pan, and roasted it in the oven slowly till it was cooked through and a half inch of oil was in the bottom of the pan. It seems to me it was the best salmon I ever ate. He had potatoes and hot biscuits with coffee. Dave was a good cook.

We shoved off after supper and had a good night's run. Wednesday morning, at five, the night watch turned in. I woke at ten, and the day boys had a grand down wind. We were pitching and rolling, the sail was stretching under the strain, and we calculated we were making from twelve to fifteen miles per hour.

Tuesday we had passed a nice little place on a beautiful site. It had some good buildings and a church. We thought it to be Andreafsky, but that night we had pulled into The Holy Cross Mission and found we were still two hundred miles from Andreafsky. A priest there told us to be sure to keep to the right hand side of the river when we approached the delta, as we would get lost in any other than the right hand channel or delta. The delta of the Yukon is thirty-six miles across.

The wind and waves got so bad as we ran the middle of the stream, we decided to run into the left hand shore till the wind abated. The river here we thought to be five to six miles wide, or even more, one solid current. When we stood on the left shore, we could see only the tops of the trees on the opposite bank, and looking down or up stream was like looking out on the ocean.

We tied up at the left shore till after supper. Then, the wind having gone down some, we decided to cross to the right side so we shouldn't miss the right hand channel. The waves were still high, and we would have to be careful not to get in the trough of the waves, or we might be capsized. We planned to row diagonally up stream,

158

that is, diagonal with the waves. The current and wind would carry us down; but we should keep the boat angling the waves to mid-stream, then on top of a wave, wheel and head diagonally to the other shore.

Four of the boys were at the oars and one on the sweep. I was to tend the sail and, at the proper moment, run it up. It worked like a charm. At mid-stream, we selected the wave to turn on and, as we mounted its top, we all shouted, "Turn!" We wheeled beautifully, I ran up the sail and away we went driving toward the right shore.

We had good running during the night, and in the morning, after breakfast, we came to a large stream, a big river in itself, breaking off to the right, and we felt sure it was the right hand channel. We ran into it. As we entered, running along its left bank close to heavy timber, a few geese were making a noise just above the tree tops. I thought they might come over us and picked up a gun. Just then two of them came out over us, and I aimed at one of them; but the rocking of the boat threw me off twice, and just as the last one was going back over the trees again, they all yelled, "Shoot! Shoot!" I got my aim again and pulled. That goose came straight down and just missed the boat.

That was a minor incident; we had been having all the ducks we wanted. I never saw so many water fowl. One could shoot them passing the boat any time. But we were in for something far more serious.

We ran down that current at a good rate of speed. As it turned right and left like a snake, we found it breaking over its banks and disappearing into great swamps. Every divurgent stream reduced the size of the main stream, and we became alarmed. We expected the water to join us again farther down but it never did. Our stream got smaller and smaller and toward evening we ran slab-dab into a log jamb that completely barred our progress. We were up against it proper, at least thirty miles from the river, lost in a blind slough. How could we ever pull that thirty foot boat back to the main stream! It looked impossible.

Away off to the right, a range of hills formed a half circle; and it looked like the swamp reached to them. Having to leave our boat there and try to go on foot or swim was an appalling thought. Would we be lost in the swamp? We were all very grave, and said little for a long while.

I had been looking at the mountains to the left, in the direction the main river must be, and so had Dave. I finally said, "Boys, that break in the mountains ahead looks like the river went through there. If this log jamb were not here, we should come out on the river again a short distance ahead, perhaps half a mile. The water we started with surely finds the main stream again. It couldn't be otherwise. I propose two of us go over this jamb and find out. If it proves so, we may find some way to move enough logs to let us through, or find some way to get the boat over the jamb."

Dave said, "I second the motion. I think the same thing, and Bob and I will go." I said, "We'll do it."

"No, no!" came a chorus from the others. "You'll get lost, and then we'll be fixed right."

No amount of argument would persuade them. They proposed we get a good sleep and in the morning tackle the back track. It seemed impossible to reach the river again with the boat, but one of them said, "All in favor of hitting the back track in the morning say 'I'." The vote was four to two, and we prepared to spend the night right there with the mosquitoes!

After supper, four of the boys got out on a mossy knoll, set up mosquito bar on sticks, and crawled under. I sat up against the back of the boat with my gloves on, the bar all fixed. Duncan spread the sail out and rolled up in that. I was afraid he would smother. I didn't sleep a wink. I was worried. I put in a good part of the night thinking of the folks back home, and what a calamity it would be if we disappeared right there.

I must have sent telepathic waves to my wife, for she said to me a few days after we got home, "Where were you, and what happened to you about the twenty-second or twenty-third of June? I didn't sleep all night and just knew you were in trouble." I got my note-book and found we were there in that swamp.

Came the morning, we got a good early start and were favored in two ways. The boat drew only five or six inches of water, and the swamp alongside of our stream was formed of stretches of lakes, some of them two to three miles long. By getting into them at their lower ends, we had practically still water to pull through.

It broke our hearts to leave our birch bark canoe down there, but there was no recourse. We cut it adrift before we started and bid it good-bye.

We got along nicely for some hours. We negotiated several of the little lakes and got back into the stream again. But as we proceeded, our getting back into the stream was hampered more and more by trees growing in the inlets of these lakes. We finally ran up against quite a bunch of these little trees, six to eight inches thick at the water top. We couldn't get the boat between them. Dave took an ax, and, hooking his leg over the prow of the boat, he chopped one of those trees off below the water sufficiently to let us slide the boat over. We took turns at that exercise and got through but soon had enough of it. From then on we kept to the stream.

We zigzagged back and forth as the stream bent, keeping to the quieter side and shooting across the stream at the bends, five men on the oars and one on the sweep. Worn out, we reached the main river at nine that evening. What a relief! I hadn't thought we could ever do it.

Some distance below, near what is called on my present map, Fortuna Ledge, we came to another strong stream going off to the right, but we had had our lesson.

We were drifting along pleasantly below that outlet, about where my present map is marked Pilot, when we saw two Indians in a canoe. Dave called to them, "Got any fish?"

"Yah."

Dave waved them to come along side. He remarked, "Got fish, we buy." One of them handed him a salmon. Dave laid it on the side of the boat and said to us, "I can't tell whether this is a King salmon or not. It looks like it might be a dog or white salmon. If they would let me cut it across the back, I could tell by the color." He took a knife and tried to make them understand he would like to cut it. They nodded, apparently giving consent. He cut into the fish about an inch and passed it back saying, "It's a dog salmon. Got any more?" They passed up another, and he cut it. It was a dog salmon also. The Indians looked at us quizzically about two minutes, then letting loose of our boat they struck their paddles and shot out to shore. There was not another Indian, nor canoe, nor village in sight.

About half way to shore, they let out a terrific whoop, and before one could say "Jack Robinson," there shot out of the willows about fifty canoes! One and two Indians in each canoe. We were startled.

They formed a circle about us, and when the circle was complete, they yelled tauntingly at us. We could see them plainly shove shells into rifles and, as they did this, they pointed the guns at us and pointed down into the water. They were going to sink us! They could do it all right, and no one would know where we had disappeared. We could see that at once. It was a very grave situation.

They kept going around us in a circle and getting closer, Finally, I thought close enough to reach with buck shot from a shot gun. We didn't have a rifle. I lifted a shot gun from the nails on the side of the boat, pulled out a box of shells, put two in the barrels, threw my loaded revolver over to Duncan, and remarked, "The first blankety blank that fires on us will get a load of buckshot!"

We sat tense, bewildered. The goose pimples raised on my neck. A minute, two minutes passed. They did not fire, and Dave rose to the occasion, as usual. He stood up and selected the Indian he thought to be the chief or leader. His hunch was right. He raised his hand and yelled at him, "Got any fish?"

"Huh?"

"Got any fish?"

"Yah," in a disinterested voice.

"Bring here, we buy."

They poised their paddles, seemingly undecided. Dave made a couple more attempts, and they, the two in the canoe addressed, came in, the other canoes held their positions, paddles poised.

As Dave took the first fish up over the side he remarked, "This is a King salmon!" Then turning to the Indian he said, "How much?"

The Indian said, "Half dollar."

Dave passed him a half dollar, and said, "Got any more?" Another salmon was passed up, and Dave gave him another half dollar.

The instant the first half dollar was passed, that ring of canoes broke and disappeared quickly among the willows along the shore. What a relief passed through us! "If we never see them again it will be too soon."

The Chief hung to our boat quite a distance and wanted to talk. He could speak fair English after his deal was concluded satisfactorily. He finally enlightened us with this bit of information, "Me, Pilot!"

"Oh, you're a Pilot?" Dave queried. "Yah, me Pilot."

"Whom do you pilot for?" "Pak. comp." (Packing Companies)

"How far do you pilot their boat?"

"Two hunnerd mile."

"Well, well! That's a nice job."

"Yah, me pilot two year."

He left, and I am glad to say we did not see him again.

XXIV

WE HIT THE SWELLS

The next day as we were drifting along, we met our first kayak, a canoe made from the skins of the seal stretched over a frame. The Yukon has three kinds of canoes: the dugout, the birch-bark, and kayak. They seem to belong to their respective parts of the river and are all skillfully made.

This kayak had two openings in its top. The openings are circular and have a coaming or hoop collar around the opening. There were two Eskimos in this canoe. They wore opaque waterproof skin coats that fit closely around the face, went over the head, down over their arms and bodies, fit tight around the wrists, and lastly, were tied about the coaming. No wave beating over could find entrance to the wearers or get into the canoe. The kayak and coat make a wonderful combination.

These fellows paddled up to us, and reaching up, held on to our boat and drifted with us quite a while. They had beautiful faces, a clear yellowish skin with rosy cheeks and large black eyes. I grunted and made signs to them, but no sign of understanding came from them. They neither grunted or made signs in return. They just stared like two owls. I think they may have been two boys from sixteen to twenty years old.

Vochs said, "I think they are squaws."

I turned to them and said, "You squaws?" I said it several times, but got no sign of understanding in return, and I didn't know the word for 'woman' in the Eskimo language.

Vochs said, "Bob, would you shoot buckshot into faces like that?"

"I would shoot into anything that shot me," I replied.

We soon passed Andreafsky, and our next excitement was to be the Bering Sea. I was on the sweep all that night, but we did not reach the sea. Expecting to reach

164

it any time, I made the foolish announcement, "I will not sleep till I see the sea!" I was on the sweep all day and was due for the night watch again, making three shifts straight. Of course, one of the boys would have taken my place, but I had resolved to stay on that sweep "till we reached the sea."

After supper, I took the sweep again, and we were tearing along before a good wind. At nine o'clock, we suddenly rounded a bend and there before us we beheld a narrow, short cut between two high clay banks, and just beyond, the breakers and swells of the sea.

Had those parties up river told us not to turn out till we had the sea in full view, that the right channel was short, and the sea should be seen clearly before taking any right hand channel, it would have saved us from getting into the swamps. Saved us much time and worry.

"What ho!" We were being pulled through that clay cut by the sail and current at an ever increasing rate of speed.

Several yelled, "Pull in!" "Pull in!"

"Pull in where?" There was nothing but high clay banks to pull to. The right hand bank was about thirty feet straight up out of the water and nothing to tie to.

They yelled above the noise, "We can't run into those breakers!"

"O.K. Let the sail down!" I yelled back.

One fellow jumped to lower the sail, and I turned the boat to lay it along side the clay wall, prow up stream, as the only chance. But the rope was tangled and he couldn't let the sail drop at the proper moment, and we banged head on into that clay wall. Every one was staggered or knocked down. Just then, we heard a great yell of laughter over head, and looking up on top of the clay bank, there was a crowd of Eskimos laughing fit to kill. It was funny. We were laughing, too.

A couple of the boys jabbed sticks into the wall to steady us while we planned what to do. The first advisors proclaimed we should camp till there was a calm, and the

waves went down. It was a new and terrifying sight to
five of us. A half mile or more of black quivering mud,
as the breakers receded, was exposed on both sides of
the channel which was marked by painted pilings. The
next wave sent its breakers rolling up over that mud-flat
like they were coming to get us. We had some forty to
fifty miles to go over that sea before we could enter the
channel behind Michael's Island, or we could walk. Walking, of course, was out of the question. The shore was
not a likely place to enjoy a walk. It seemed for a while
like we were all in favor of camping till the sea quieted
down. But Dave, the only one of us who had sea experience, had said nothing. Then he spoke up, "No, don't let
us camp! Now is the time to hit it while we have a good
wind. We might be here two weeks before those swells go
down. There are no white caps, and this boat will ride
those swells like a top."

We looked at Dave, but he meant it. We looked at
those breakers and shuddered. Then, "All right, Dave,
you're the doctor."

We turned the boat about and ran up the sail. We
headed for those breakers. I was on the sweep and shot
the boat down the middle of those pilings. And I want to
confess that I never had, before nor since, such a coat of
goose flesh. The chills and sweats alternated up and
down my back. The mud flat on both sides quivered, and
ahead came the next breaker. We got a good head of
speed. As we hit that breaker, we went up into the air
in a cloud of spray, jumping half out of the water, and
landing with a resounding slap on the other side. I was
staggered by the impact, as I stood in the rear with the
sweep end under my arm and hung on for dear life. We
were out on the swells before the next breaker formed
and escaped with only one of those playful things. After
riding two or three swells, I recovered my breath. We
could do it, as Dave said.

I kept the boat hitting the swells at right angles, but
as that ran us out to sea and the shore of the bay ran

away off to the right, there was soon a clamor not to get out so far from the shore. I angled a little to the right but not enough to get into the hollow of the waves.

After about a half hour's running, we sighted, ahead, a big rounded something. "It's a whale!" "It's a big log!" were some of the comments. We saw it only as often as we reached the top of the swells.

Finally Dave said, "I think that is the top of a mountain."

"Away out there?" we asked.

"We'll see." He got the map and sure enough, it was Point Romanoff. "That's about forty miles away on the other side of the bay." he said. Then, to me, "Steer straight for it." It took us farther from shore, but I laid the prow at it and away we went.

When we got used to the running up and running down, three of the boys lay down to sleep. It was my third shift, but I was having too much fun to think of sleep. Dave and Vochs took the oars to warm up, as it got kind of chilly. Dave was a skilled oarsman, but Vochs was powerful and was on the seaside oar. He went at it like mad, and though I cranked the sweep against him, we were soon in the trough of the waves. The wind and sea were making an awful noise.

They looked at me and yelled, "Keep her out of the trough!"

I pointed to the sweep and they could see I could do no more. I had it jambed clear over. It was their uneven pulling that was doing the damage. Vochs let up awhile, and we came around all right. After that they struck an even stroke.

We had been running about four hours. About one o'clock a. m., Duncan awoke and sat up. He could just look over the side of the boat. After looking at the swells a few minutes, he looked around at me standing in the stern with the sweep under my arm. The noise was deafening. Then he yelled, "Hadn't we better run in?"

I gave him the laugh, and yelled back, "Been doing this four hours, it's all right." Waking out of his sleep, he thought it terrible, no doubt. He sat there looking over the side about five minutes, then lay down and rolled up in the blankets and went to sleep.

Three hours later, as we were rounding Point Roman-off, where the waves roared on the rocks and flew into the air in spray one hundred feet high, the boys woke up. We were compelled to angle the waves to round the point and were dancing the worst yet, to the loudest music. I didn't blame them for waking under the circumstances. Soon after rounding the point we came to a little bay where the water was still.

They yelled, "Let's run in there for breakfast." I felt relieved, and turned the boat in. As it grated upon the gravel shore, I dropped the sweep and took a header into that bunk. I did not know anything more till two p. m. I had slept nine and a half hours and was awakened by a yell.

We were in a beautiful bay; that is, the water was still. The country about was low and level, but no trees or bushes. I rose to see what the yelling was about and found we were near a large ocean going steamer at anchor; and one of the boys was calling to a solitary man on its deck, to learn where the entrance to the canal was that ran through, and made Michaels Island.

Pointing beyond his steamer, he said, "Right over there, but the ebb tide has set in, and I would advise you to stay here till the flood tide. It will take you through much easier. It would be a big job bucking the tide." We thanked him and said we would take a look at the canal. Why that man was alone on that steamer, is still a mystery.

While I had slept, the boys had breakfast and came up shore to the bay from which the Michaels canal begins. That canal is a unique thing. It looks like Paul Bunyan had taken his big shovel and ripped it across sixteen or seventeen miles. It is, for the most part, I'll guess, ten to twenty yards wide. I will also guess that at some distant past, the sea bottom gave way, letting that broad flat peninsula sink a little, and cracked the land across. The tides flow in and out its entire length, forming the point of the peninsula into an island, called Michaels Island.

The whole big flat seems to be lava with a kind of moss and grass covering. The origin of the lava is evident in the three extinct volcanoes to the north. The channel does not seem to be deep. At the St. Michaels end, where we later arrived at low tide, we found hardly enough water to pull the boat through the scattering of big black blocks of lava on the bottom.

We rowed around the steamer and found the entrance to the canal. The tide was beginning to run out, but the boys were feeling strong and restless and decided to buck it. Five men took the oars and I the sweep as usual. I don't know why I was on the sweep the whole length of the Yukon, but I do know that the boys must have had considerable confidence in my steering the night before, when they slept seven hours while I piloted the boat through those swells.

We began fighting that tide about two-thirty p. m. We fought it for about fifteen miles; getting relief from its current some mile or two from the Michaels end. We not only fought tide, we fought mosquitoes. They drove Vochs crazy again.

I didn't tell of his fights with the mosquitoes coming down the river. On the calm days, when we had no wind to keep them away, they were fierce. Vochs slept days. He would lie on his side to go to sleep and soon his breath would dampen his mosquito bar and it would fall on his cheek. Immediately the whole of his cheek was black. Mosquitoes a half inch thick, all trying to get their bills into him at once. He would toss in his sleep a few times and shake them off, but they were upon him again.

When he could stand it no longer, he would roll on his back. He would get about a minute's relief, when his bar would sag again and rest on his nose. Then they pounced on the end of his nose and built themselves up in a pile like a black walnut.

In desperation and still asleep, he would claw at his nose and off would come his whole mosquito bar, hat and all. Then the howling dervishes would attack. They filled his face and neck and nostrils, forcing him to awake, which was terrible for he had lost so much sleep because of them. He would sit up and fight them and cuss them, his eyes rolling like an infuriated bull and the froth running from the corners of his mouth. For a few minutes the man was mentally unbalanced. They surely went for him. No other one of us attracted them as much as he did.

These insects circle about one's head from right to left always. The circle is about two to three feet in diameter, and a foot thick. The center six to eight inches is so dense one can not see through it. Desiring to see each other, two persons must lower or raise their heads suddenly and peer below or above the circle. Their high keyed buzz or war whoop is continuous the whole summer. When two persons come closer together than three feet, the two circles unite and form an ellipse about the two heads and go on with the blood-curdling dance.

XXV

BERING SEA AND PACIFIC

We reached St. Michaels at ten-thirty p. m. We were about eight hours negotiating the crack in the ground. Some seventeen miles, nearly two miles an hour. We did not stop a minute on the way and that was good time, tide considered.

It was June 27, and we were sixteen and a half days from Dawson. We figured up our lost time along the way and found we had actually run the eighteen hundred and fifty miles in fourteen days, or an average of about one hundred and twenty-nine miles per day. We were tired out, of course. We ran into shore, tied up, had some supper, and all turned in till next day.

St. Michael's consisted of a long shed or two used as warehouses by shipping interests. I think there was a little house or two besides the sheds, that was all. Back inland about a quarter of a mile, there was an Eskimo village of about two to four hundred people.

There were eleven schooners and two steamers anchored before the town. The schooners were unloaded, but the steamers had not begun to unload. The schooners might go south any time, the steamers, in about two weeks. We would ship on a schooner if we could.

We were camped there till 8:00 o'clock p. m., June 30. While spending the three days, we had only one diversion. A one-hole kayak was tied up near us, and a quite fat, well-dressed white man noticing it, decided to get into it. He brought it close to a large, rounded boulder that stuck up out of the water. Carefully, he put one foot into the hole of the canoe while resting his weight on his other foot on the boulder; but the moment he tried to put his weight on the foot in the kayak, it commenced to buck. He drew back and repeated the performance. That kayak would have none of him. He tried to get both feet in for perhaps half an hour. He finally made a desperate

171

attempt, so did the kayak, and over he went into the water, getting properly soused. After he was wet and mad, he was more determined than ever to climb in; and, standing in the water, he put a foot into the boat. But every time it bucked him out. He wore himself out and gave it up. It was not a white man's boat.

A little later, along came the Eskimo. He stepped over on the boulder, drew the little thing gently along side, and in one dextrous movement, he slid into the hole and onto the bottom. The boat had hardly made a quiver. He picked up his paddle and was soon out of sight up the shore. We were interested and amused.

I was often entertained by reading Mark Twain's "Eskimo Sweetheart," but I may have been nearer to an Eskimo sweetheart than Mark. He imagined himself sitting with her on a block of ice but I really got within one hundred and fifty yards of mine. It happened thus: I was sitting on the shore near our boat at St. Michaels, mending my shoe, when a shadow fell across my work; and looking up, there stood an Eskimo boy about twelve years old.

"Hello," I said.

"Hello," he replied.

"Where do you live?"

"Over there," he replied, pointing over to the Eskimo village.

"Got any family?" I asked.

"Yes."

"How many in your family?"

"One brother, three sisters, father and mother."

"Oh, you have three sisters, have you?"

"Yes."

"How old are your sisters?"

"One six, one fourteen and one eighteen."

"You have a sister eighteen? Is she good looking?"

"I don't know. I guess so."

I went on quizzing him in an offhand manner just to be agreeable. We talked about anything that happened to come up. Then, as I got my shoe finished, I put it on and rose to put my repair kit in the boat. As I did so, my young friend moved away, and thoughtlessly, I handed him this old chestnut: "Say, tell your oldest sister to meet me here tonight at twelve o'clock." In the States, that would have been a laughing parting; but I did not understand the Eskimo seriousness, and he did not understand my foolishness.

All this left my mind at once as other things came up; but I awoke that night, and as was my habit, I pulled out my watch to see the time. It was a few minutes before midnight, and quite light, of course, and the first thing that came to my mind was my conversation with that boy, and what I had said to him as he went away. Cautiously, I rose and peeked over the edge of the boat, and what do you suppose I saw? A young Eskimo girl hurrying to the highest point of ground about one hundred and fifty yards from the boat. It gave me a shock.

My foolishness had caused that young lady to lose her sleep and come out there at midnight. She stopped on the high point and searched our neighborhood with her eyes. I ducked. I did not have nerve enough to go over and apologize. I looked over the edge of the boat again in about five minutes and she was gone. I can plainly see her yet as she stopped. She was dressed in a calico dress, with a full sized apron. As she stopped, the chilly breeze fluttered her gown and she tucked her hands up under her apron for warmth.

We had been held up here about three days when one of the boys came and told us we could get passage on a schooner pulling out for Seattle the next day, for fifty dollars each. But the Captain assured him there were no passenger accommodations, and we would have to put up with board bunks and furnish our own bedding. He would not take more than ten men, but if he could get that many, he would have the ship's carpenter put in the bunks. However, we should eat at the same table with him.

We found four of our outfit would go. Brown and Lorenz decided to wait for the steamer. We notified the Captain four of us would like to be booked among that ten. He readily found six more, and we were all set to go aboard June 30.

During the day, I became acquainted with a man from Australia. He was broke but had hopes of reaching Dawson. He wanted to know what we were going to do with our boat, as he would like to have it. I told him he might have it, I would see. I got the signatures of the four who were leaving to a paper, giving him our share, and Brown and Lorenz said they would sign when the steamer they went on pulled out. I presume he got the boat and hope he found it an assistance in his far travels.

In the afternoon, I found Brown changing his clothes for a nice new suit he had been saving in his luggage. I asked him what he was going to do with the old suit. He said, "Throw it in the sea." I said, "Not much, I'll take it." I changed mine for it right then and there and threw mine into the sea. Brown's suit wasn't much, but mine was much less. A good part of both was left scattered the length of the Yukon.

The schooner's boat came for the ten passengers at eight o'clock. We were all from Dawson, all miners, and had all come down the Yukon in small boats. We were called the ten miners by the crew of the schooner. The Captain took us down the hold and showed us our beds. You would laugh, but we were satisfied. We had been having every imaginable hard bed the past year and thought nothing of the Captain's new bunks.

They were just plain board boxes nailed to uprights, one above the other, four high. Two foot boards for bottoms and six inch boards for sides. Our mattresses were the two foot boards, and, to keep them from pinching as the boat rolled, we put a piece of canvas or sail cloth on the boards. As the boat rolled, one board sank under our weight, then on the return roll, the other board sank. We were "Rocked in the Cradle of the Deep."

BERING SEA AND PACIFIC

July first there was a little wind. They raised anchor and we moved off two miles, when the wind left us, and there we stuck till the next day at noon. We had some time trying to run the six or seven hundred miles of Bering Sea, depending on the wind. It took us nineteen days to get out of that frog pond.

But I am getting ahead of my story. The West Indies cook the Captain had on the up trip had taken sick at Michaels, and the Captain had secured the services of a little wiry old Scotch American.

Jimmy was a good cook. He was also a hard case. He gave us good grub for about three days, then he began to slight the cooking and variety. At first, we thought the blame lay with the Captain but learned he was dissatisfied, as well as us. Jimmy not only got lazy on the job, but sassy and overbearing. He would say, "Bob" or "Dave" whoever it happened to be, "Go down the hold and bring me a pail of water, or sack of potatoes" or whatever it happened he needed. We were all willing to help, but he got so cranky he would tell us to "Get the hell out of the galley" if we stopped to take a drink from the pail of water after we brought it up for him.

Finally, the boys all refused to bring him anything, and Jimmy practically quit cooking, told us if we didn't like it to "Go to hell." This went on till the seventh, and got rapidly worse. Then we miners held a meeting down the hold and sent a committee with our complaint to the Captain.

He said, "Boys, I have contracted Jimmy as cook to Port Townsend, and though he doesn't suit me, I can't discharge him, for I'll have to pay him for the whole trip. Besides I have no one to take his place."

We assured him his colored cook was again quite well and would take the job over if we boys would help him, which we had agreed to do if we could get Jimmy removed. Besides, we could all cook and wouldn't see the job undone.

175

The Captain said, "I'll tell you, if we could get him to quit, I would not be responsible, and your proposition would suit me. You boys go down the hold, and after awhile, come up again all in a body. I'll meet you before the galley door, and you make your demands so Jimmy can hear you. We shall see what he will do."

The committee came back down the hold and reported. We made arrangements to go up and appointed a spokesman.

The Captain came along and met us at the galley door, and our spokesman said, "Captain, we miners have held a meeting and decided that we want better cooking, or we want you to land us on the shore."

"Why," the Captain said, "doesn't the cooking suit you?"

"No, it doesn't, nor the cook neither,"—with much more.

Jimmy was listening and came blustering out. "A miner's meeting on the high seas!" he laughed. Then, "Is there any one of you capable of the job?"

"Sure, we can all cook."

"Then here's your damn galley!" He threw off his apron and cap and walked out, laughingly sarcastic, as he remarked, "A miner's meeting on the high seas!" As he walked out, Dave and the colored cook walked in, and, say, we had good grub the remainder of the trip. I washed dishes to Port Townsend.

That Bering Sea trip was monotonous compared with the river trip. We amused ourselves as best we could. Some of the boys played poker and quarreled a little. The funniest part of the poker playing affected the Captain. He was a big Norwegian-American and had been married just before leaving Seattle. His wife was awaiting his return. He got into the poker games and owed all the boys when they got through.

A tall Texan, Jim, I forget his last name, the only one of us who struck it rich in the diggings, was sore at the Captain because he borrowed from him so much. He sold the Captain a pair of blankets and told us he was going to get even with him. He said, "Those blankets are full of gray-backs, and I am trying to imagine Captain and his new wife when they get into them."

We had lots of fresh water on board, but as a precautionary measure Captain would not let us use any of it to wash in till we were safely near our port. As a result, we washed in salt water, and every wash seemed to put on another coat of salt. We were afraid to laugh lest our faces would crack open.

Many things of interest came to our attention: a pet gull, a pet seal, with their antics. Many little things we land-lubbers had never seen helped while away the weary days.

In rough weather most of the boys and several of the sailors became sea sick. Duncan and I never did, and never missed a meal.

The morning of the nineteenth, at breakfast, the Captain said, "We shall hit the pass at ten o'clock, the Unimak Pass, in the Alaska Peninsula." At ten o'clock, we were a half-mile from land, but no pass in sight. Captain ordered the anchor over and we came to a stop. He and the First Mate anxiously scanned the shore with glasses. In fact, they had been scanning the shore ever since we sighted land, and only a close mountain range, with no pass, was before us. They had missed the pass.

We were interested in a smoking volcano, and hundreds of whales, while we lay there at anchor. Those whales were monstrous animals, nearly as long as the ship, which was only one hundred and twenty-five feet long.

We lay there four hours while Captain and the Mate figured out their position, and what to do. The whales were about our only amusement. There were some spouting continually, as far as we could look. Each, taking its turn rising for air, after a few minutes below feeding, let go its spout.

At two o'clock p. m. Captain ordered the anchor raised and the boat turned completely about. The sail was all spread, and we headed back into the sea. We were still going back when we went to sleep that night. At two a.m. we were all awakened by the changing sail, and we were turned about once more and headed for the Peninsula. At ten a.m. we hit the Pass fairly in the middle. I considered that a piece of nice work. They sailed back twelve hours, then forward eight hours, striking the Pass fairly and at a time when the light was strong.

As we entered the Pass, a strong wind seemed to suck through there and took us a kiting into the Pacific. That wind never left us till we reached Cape Flattery, seventeen hundred miles. It varied at times, but we were always running ahead of it, "Ving a Ving" as the Captain would say—spread sails both ways. We made the seventeen hundred miles in eight days. That was more like it and I enjoyed that sail. At times the sea swept the decks. I liked to hang to the upper rail and raise my feet as the seas came swashing by.

One day, when it was not rough, the Mate came up to take the time from the sun. As we were crossing the Meridian, he did this every day; but this day, I asked him if I could take a peep through the sextant. And I would urge every one who gets a chance to take a look through one. He handed me the sextant, told me to look at the sun and when it sank half deep in the sea, to yell, "Twelve o'clock." The sun was then at what seemed to me to be its highest, and I wondered at his remark. But placing my eye to the telescope, what was my surprise to see the sun close to the sea on the horizon. And it was moving quite rapidly along the water, getting lower and lower, till it touched and sank into the water. When it buried itself half down, I yelled, "Twelve o'clock!" and a sailor down below rang the bell. This may seem childish to sailors who are familiar with the sextant, but to me it was a wonderful experience which I still cherish.

BERING SEA AND PACIFIC

One day the swells were breaking only up against the prow and didn't come over the deck. I was standing near the man at the wheel, and two of the boys were standing up against the forward rail. The wheelman said, with a grin, "Watch me douse those boys," As the swell came tearing in, he gave the wheel a quick turn, causing the ship to turn slightly and the swell came over the forward rail, breaking into spray that sprinkled the boys and made them run for safety. They never knew how it happened; thought it an accident, I suppose.

We always had some large birds, like buzzards, sailing about. I asked a sailor what the bird was and he said, "A Gooney." At that time I did not know what a Gooney was but later learned that the albatross which inhabits certain islands of the Pacific is called a Gooney.

The sailor said to me, "I'll bet if you throw anything overboard any time before he gets out of sight, he will see it." The bird was sailing close to the water and going swiftly behind us. The sailor stepped into the galley and came out with a piece of bread. The bird was away back there apparently intent on reaching Siberia, paying no attention to us. The sailor stood by the rail as though he figured the bird was too far off to get a fair chance, but by and by, to my amazement, he threw the bread just over the side. Instantly, that bird wheeled about and came toward us. I couldn't believe he had seen that bread, and I watched him till he came to the bread and lit on the water beside it and ate it. Such eyesight I had never seen!

We reached Cape Flattery, and I was thrilled to be the first one to see land and thought of the man who shouted to Columbus, on seeing America, "Land, Land!"

The wind behind us carried us into the strait of Juan deFuca about a half mile, then left us flat. In the next two days, we had occasion to learn why that cape was christened' Flattery.' The wind flattered us till we got started in the Strait, then with a giggle in the sails, left

179

us flat—just like that. The hussy! After being our sweetheart so long.

We rolled out on the falling tide, a mile or two, then on flood tide, we rolled in again. Back and forth, all night, next day, next night and next day. Tugs came out and pulled other schooners past us almost as soon as they arrived, but we sulked back and forth, showing the disgrace we felt.

XXVI

HOME!

We reached the Strait July twenty-seventh at five-thirty. After lolling in and out for a night and day, and seeing tugs come out and pick up other schooners and run off down the Strait, we became uneasy. What made us more uneasy, the sailors told us Cape Flattery was the graveyard of the coast; many ships were wrecked there.

We went to see the Captain and complained. He said it would cost him from sixty to seventy-five dollars to be towed in, and he could not afford it. But if we boys would contribute five dollars each, he would stand the difference and call the next tug. We agreed and told him to get busy.

Tugs came out with ships, and went in with ships, that night and all next day; but we sulked. We went to the Captain again in the evening to learn why he let all those tugs pass, and he said, "Vell, I ketch da next one." Just after supper, a tug came out the Strait, and we notified the Captain and he said, "Aw right, now you fellers go below out of sight; if they see a bunch of miners on board they vill soak me plenty."

There was a large six-masted schooner lying behind us. It had just come up a couple of hours before. Captain ran up the flag for the tug; they spoke to him as they ran by and told him they would pick up both ships. The tug ran out to the other boat and attached a howser, then came toward us, paying out line till one would think they would run out of rope. As they passed us, our sailors hooked the line and pulled it on board and made it fast, and away we went. The tug, trailing both boats, far apart, started down the Strait. The moon came out full and clear. The air was so warm and balmy, it made us all feel good. The boys began to sing, and, running around, I found a sailor who had an accordion. I borrowed it and began marching around the deck, playing a march. The

181

boys all fell in, and we marched and sang. Then half the boys tied white bands around their arms. They were women for the time being, and they all danced while I played waltzes, quadrilles, schottisches and polkas. What a stag dance they had! The air, moon and water were perfect; and the shore lights flashed on and off.

The next morning, we were passing a ghost city on the right. Looked like it should have a population of three to four thousand, but not a soul in sight! I asked a sailor if he knew anything about it and he said, "That is Port Angeles. It was a boom town; and I think only a man or two are left to care for it. Everybody else moved away." I understand it has boomed again and is quite a city.

We anchored off Townsend at 2:30 p. m., July 30. They lowered a boat, and we all climbed down the rope ladder into it and pulled to shore. After settling up with the Captain, we made our way to the dock where we took a boat for Seattle. Dave, Duncan and I were still together. At the dock, we met a fraternal brother who was much interested in the Klondike, and we talked with him all the way around the Sound.

Duncan and I told him we did not know how we would spend the night as we were without money except gold dust; and, as the next day was Sunday, we likely could not get cash till Monday morning. He told us a U. S. assay office had been opened at Seattle, and we could turn in our gold there Monday. In the meantime, he would take us to a place to put up. Dave knew of a place he could stay and would raise some cash and let us have some in the morning. We got into Seattle at 11:00 p. m., and would have had to stay at the dock till morning only for our newly found Lodge brother.

He was a business man of Seattle, about thirty years old. I am sorry I don't find his name in my note book because he did us a good turn. When we landed, he took up a diagonal street that ran from the docks, I think in a north-easterly direction. There were side-walks only on the right hand side of the street. We walked up the gentle grade of the street eleven blocks, and crossed over to a two or three story cottage style, frame hotel.

Every one seemed to be in bed, but a few rings brought the proprietor. They called each other by their first names; and our friend said, "Here are a couple friends of mine just came in on the boat from Klondike, and I would like you to put them up till the assay office opens Monday, when they will have money. Don't mind their appearance, they have been through the rough but are all right." The hotel man said he would surely put us up.

We were looking about as tough as it is possible to look; two months' whiskers, hair sticking from several holes in our hats, weather-beaten to a finish, our clothes in rags, elbows, knees and seats out, and dirty.

Our friend bid us good-night, and we never saw him again. We told the proprietor we had no bugs, but we were so dirty we did not want him to give us a bed, just a blanket on the floor, till we got cleaned up.

"That's all right boys, come with me." He took us up stairs and into, I think, his best room, with two beds so clean and white, we objected. "No, you don't!" he said, "You are going to make yourselves at home right here! Good-night."

We both undressed and rolled into one bed, leaving the other clean, but we didn't sleep. The bed was too still. We had been used to holding on to the side of the bunk on ship-board, while we were rolled back and forth and slept soundly all the while. That tame bed, so soft and clean, was out of our ken. As daylight appeared, we dozed a bit, but the sun came through the windows to stop that. Duncan got up first, washed and dressed, and said, "Well, aren't you going to get up?"

"What for?" I queried.

"To get some breakfast, of course," he said.

"Have you the price?" I asked.

He looked at me a moment, and, grinning, pulled off his clothes and rolled back into bed.

183

I lay there and thought, "It's hell to have several hundred dollars in one's pocket and can't get a breakfast." Finally, my thick head generated a bright idea. I got up, washed and dressed.

His Nibs looked at me with a grin and said, "Now, what do you think you are going to do?"

"Oh, I am just going out for a walk," I replied.

I went down the street nearly to the dock, then the center of the city. I passed a restaurant a n d looked through the window. A couple of doors farther along I found what I was looking for—a jewelry store—and the door was open. A nice old man came forward to wait on me.

"Do you buy gold dust?" I asked.

"Sometimes, where is it from?"

"Eldorado and Bonanza creeks, Klondike."

"I have some here from those creeks."

He brought down a silver bowl from the shelf; it contained about two or three hundred dollars. I pointed out the red was Bonanza gold while the yellow was Eldorado.

"Could you buy an ounce?"

"Yes."

"What can you pay?"

"About fifteen dollars and seventy-five c e n t s a n ounce."

"We got in last night at eleven p. m., and need to eat today. If you can buy an ounce, we'll eat." I gave him our sack, and as he took it, I got another idea from the cobwebs.

"How much could you buy?" I asked.

"Oh, it doesn't matter, I'm safe at $15.75."

"Well, let's see, weigh out four ounces."

He weighed out four ounces, and gave me sixty-three dollars, in fives, ones, and twos.

Then I asked, "Where could we get a couple of tailor-made suits by tomorrow night?"

HOME!

"Don't you do it! See this suit I have on? It cost about a third the price of a tailor-made, and the stores are all open here till noon."

After some talk, I went out, and back to the restaurant and had a good breakfast. I then started up to the hotel to get Duncan. About two blocks ahead, I saw him coming.

I could see he was in a Round-up frame of mind for he pulled his long mustache first on one side and spit, then on the other side and spit, looking down all the while. I met him, but he didn't see me. I put my shoulder to his and pushed him off the sidewalk. He came up ready to fight, but seeing it was I, he said, "Seen anything of Dave?" Dave was to get us cash for over Sunday.

I said, "No."

"That's hell! I'm nearly starved!"

"No use being hungry," I said, as I opened my trousers pocket and exposed the end of my roll.

"Come on!" he roared, making several spitting sounds, as he headed for the restaurant.

We sat down at a table. The waiter came and took his order then asked me what I wanted. I said, "Nothing at all."

Duncan looked at me and asked, "What's the matter with you? Don't you want any breakfast?"

I said, "Had mine. You didn't think I could climb that hill again if I hadn't had breakfast, did you?" He laughed and never said another word till he had stowed away a T-bone and much fixings. We had not eaten since noon the day before.

We went out on the street, then he said, "Now what shall we do?"

I said, "I'll tell you. I would like to get a complete outfit of clothing, a bath, hair-cut and shave, and get rid of this dirt."

"All right," he said. "Let's go and see if we can."

We turned into a barber shop and told the barbers (there were three or four chairs) what we wanted to do.

185

They were much interested in us at once and said, "We have two bath tubs, and if you will cross the street to that furnishing store and get the outfit, we'll fix you up when you come back."

We did just that. Got a full outfit from hats to shoes; white collars and cuffs. Got a good bath, hair-cut and shave. It made some change in our appearance, as well as in our feelings.

We went out on the street and started up to the hotel to see if Dave was looking for us. We had gone just a little ways when we met Vochs. He didn't know us and Duncan shouldered him off into the ditch. Vochs came up looking so funny. He was a big, powerful fellow, nearly as tall as Duncan, near-sighted and wore glasses. He walked slowly up to Duncan who stood grinning at him. He looked and looked, and finally said, "It's not Dunk, is it?"

"You are right, as usual, Vochs."

"Well, I'll be a son-of-a-gun! I wouldn't know you in a thousand years." Then he slowly turned to me and said,

"This isn't Bob, is it?"

"Yeah! You are right again."

"Well, well, what a change!"

Just then Dave came down the street, and said he had been up to our hotel to give us some money. We assured him we would be all right till Monday, as we had made a raise.

"Well, what shall we do today?"

"Any old thing."

Then along came Texas Jim and Ed Jones, two of the ten who came down on the schooner "J.B.Leeds" with us. That made six of us together, and together we took in the town like school kids when they first pull off their shoes in spring.

What a balmy atmosphere compared with what we had been through! And how good we felt! I agreed then with that man on the dock the previous August, as we stood on the deck of the "Willamette," when he called to a friend on deck, "I know when I'm well off." He had just come from Dawson and wasn't going back till spring.

We rode all the street car lines, visited all the parks, and acted crazy in general. The town was not so big then. As evening came on, Jim said, "Boys, we'll have the last supper together. The expense is on me." We went to a restaurant, and Jim gave us a sure enough grand spread.

We never saw him again.

Monday morning, we went to the assay office and turned in our gold. Then we took a stroll. As we strolled about, we met another of the ten who came down with us. He was a Seattle carpenter, but I can't remember his name. He had his twelve year old son with him, and they were both very happy since Dad had returned from the Klondike.

Now this man was above the average in intelligence and in every way a fine man, but homely as sin. He reminded me of the man Lincoln told about. Lincoln said, "I was rushing through the brush in Southern Indiana one day, looking for a cow. I ran slapdab into another man coming in the other direction. We backed off and looked at each other, then the other fellow said, 'Stranger, I always thought I was the ugliest man in this here country, but I gin in to you.'"

I think this Seattle man was the man Lincoln met. I had an argument with him on board ship and had a grudge against him, and now I got even. He introduced me to the boy as his son. As I shook hands with the boy, I was amazed at his good looks. He was a fine specimen of handsome boyhood. I held his hand, and looking at his father, I said, "This boy must have a very beautiful mother." Everyone laughed, and the father came back with, "He has." We never saw them again.

As we had come into the Strait of Juan de Fuca, the changing climate had called up memories of the past. Such a breeze I had not felt for a year. Made one feel like he had gotten into God's country again, and I had written in my diary, "Do I feel good at seeing civilization again? Well, one in my position should know."

Our search for Klondike gold was over, and I was just about four days away from my family.

I walked into my home as my family were eating breakfast. My little four-year-old son, who had not seen me for a year, looked up at his mother with a shy smile and said, "That's him, mama, that's him."

THE END